The Consumer's Guide to Menswear

The Consumer's Guide to
MENSWEAR

Donald Dolce
WITH
Jean-Paul DeVellard

illustrations by Christopher Moser

DODD, MEAD & COMPANY

NEW YORK

LIBRARY OF CONGRESS CATALOGING IN PUBLICATION DATA:

Dolce, Donald.
    The consumer's guide to menswear.

    Includes index.
    1. Men's clothing.   2. Consumer education.
I. DeVellard, Jean-Paul.   II. Title.
TT617.D64   1983   646'32   83-1769
ISBN 0-89696-188-5 (pbk.)

Published by Dodd, Mead & Company,
79 Madison Avenue, New York, N.Y. 10016
Published simultaneously in Canada by
McClelland and Stewart Limited, Toronto
Manufactured in the United States of America
Designed by Judith Lerner
First Edition

to Mae Dolce
WHO ALWAYS HAD CONFIDENCE IN MY ABILITY
D.D.

*to Mary Jean Hughes-Magee, Mr. and Mrs. Mack Hughes,
John and Leah DeSantis, and Hal Hahn,*
WHOSE SUPPORT AND ENCOURAGEMENT
MADE MY INVOLVEMENT IN THIS PROJECT
SO MUCH MORE ENJOYABLE
J-P. D.

Contents

Acknowledgments

FOR THEIR invaluable assistance in providing information for this book, sincere thanks go to:

Robert Ward—President, Corporate Group,
  Evan-Picone
Gary Thorpe—Executive Vice-President, Robert Bruce
Norman Fryman—Executive Vice-President,
  Bidermann Industries
George Santacroce—Executive Vice-President,
  Yves St. Laurent Menswear
James Harris—B. W. Harris Outerwear
Nancy Knox—designer
Sandy Weinman—President, Ties by Sandy Weinman
William Seitz—Executive Director, New York School
  of Dry Cleaning
Douglas Crews—my able assistant at the time the book
  was written

And:

Joe Castaldo—who inspired me to write the book, and who provided continuing guidance and support. Without his help, this book would never have been written.

Introduction

SEVERAL years ago, I became alarmed at the declining overall quality in men's apparel. For so long, quality had been the key component; the menswear manufacturers and retailers prided themselves on cloth and construction of a quality far surpassing that in womenswear.

It was when inflation began in earnest in the mid-1970s that quality really began to suffer. Price became the key consideration. More and more menswear manufacturers and designers adopted the philosophy that fashion would sell a garment; quality became secondary. In fact, "fashion" in many cases became synonymous with poorer quality—a development I sorely lament.

Now, more than ever, consumers need to know how to get their money's worth in whatever they buy. However, becoming an expert in every field is impossible and impractical. *The Consumer's Guide to Menswear* is designed to make you an expert in one area; it is a handbook of the basic elements of quality to look for when buying menswear.

This is by no means a complete in-depth analysis. I have covered the key visual and common-sense points you should be aware of. Yes, much more about menswear could be documented. But for a basic consumer overview, this book will serve as an easy-to-read, easy-to-follow guide, and I almost guarantee that you will have a greater working knowledge than most store personnel selling menswear today.

I have stayed away from any fashion pronouncements or wardrobe-building tips except as they relate to quality. No one loves fashion more than I, having served as fashion merchandising director of two of the largest resident buying offices and retail consulting firms in the world. Much of my own firm's consulting work is based on discovering new fashion-oriented manufacturers. But fashion books abound, while there has never been a book devoted solely to quality in menswear.

Keep in mind that *The Consumer's Guide to Menswear* is a handbook, not a bible. Be flexible; ask questions. Armed with the information contained herein, you can't help becoming a better consumer.

DONALD DOLCE

The Consumer's Guide to Menswear

1. Suits

THE ROLE a suit plays in your wardrobe obviously depends upon your lifestyle and the kind of work you do. If your job requires or permits casual attire, you probably focus on sportswear, and see a suit as a luxury addition. If, on the other hand, yours is a more formal work atmosphere, you probably need several functional suits, and the "tailored garment" becomes the basis of your day-to-day wardrobe.

Whether you choose to wear it or simply must, a suit is the biggest investment you can make in your wardrobe. And since clothing prices have risen along with prices of everything else, and few of us have a budget that allows for impulsive or impractical buying, with suits especially our key shopping philosophy must be investment buying. Simply put, this means quality buying. Common sense tells us that a suit priced higher because of its higher quality, which should allow it to last longer, is a greater value than a lower-priced, lower-quality suit that will not last. And the way to get the highest return on your investment dollar is to know what elements constitute high quality in a suit.

THE THREE SUIT TYPES First, you should be aware that you have three basic choices when shopping for a suit: custom-made, made-to-measure, and ready-made.

From the standpoint of quality, you will find no finer suit than one that has been custom-made for you. Before a tailored-suit industry ever existed, all men's clothing was custom-made, and a man was almost as involved in the making of a suit as his tailor was. A pattern was cut expressly for him, from a fabric he had selected, and he worked on a one-to-one basis with his tailor in order to obtain a garment that not only fit perfectly but also met his aesthetic requirements.

Obviously, a customer-tailor relationship of this nature allows you to have a direct influence on quality control right at the production level. Unfortunately, however, although some custom tailoring is still being done in this country today, people skilled in this craft are few and far between, and the cost of custom tailoring has increased tremendously. A custom-made suit today might cost you anywhere from $750 to $1,300, depending on where you live and where you shop. For example, $1,300 might be considered high in, say, Topeka, but average in New York City.

If you desire a custom-made suit, and your budget permits it, by all means get one. If your tailor is good at what he does, a custom-made suit will be a sound and solid investment.

The made-to-measure suit was created by better manufacturers when the price of custom-made suits became prohibitive for many men. In essence, when you buy a made-to-measure suit, you're getting an existing suit pattern, in the size closest to your own, that can be modified to fit your particular body type more correctly. For example, if you are fairly close to a size 44 regular but your waist is considerably smaller than that of a size 44 suit, the waist will be adjusted so that the suit fits you correctly. The standard sleeve length can also be adjusted to give the suit a better fit.

A made-to-measure suit offers you a level of quality control similar to that a custom-made suit offers, and it is less expensive; you might say it's the next best thing to custom-made. It gives you an opportunity to select your suit fabric—a positive factor because it allows you some involvement in quality control. However, do not mistake a suit advertised as made-to-*order* for one that is made-to-*measure*. Made-to-order is just another term for custom-made, and that's what you pay for.

And, finally, there is the ready-made suit.

We usually think of ready-made clothing as mass-produced, coming off an assembly line like a television or a toaster. But there are assembly lines and *assembly lines*. Automobiles are also made on an assembly line, but the difference between a Mercedes and a Volkswagen is obvious. The key, of course, is the level of quality control.

At the outset of the ready-made clothing industry, there was considerable doubt as to the overall quality of a garment that had been machine-made rather than custom-made or primarily handmade. In fact, the Amal-gamated Clothing Workers Union created a grading sys-tem to tell the retailer just how much machine work had gone into the making of a tailored garment. The system worked on a scale of 8 to X—8 representing the finest ready-made suit you could buy, X indicating that vir-tually no handwork had gone into the garment. The ob-vious assumption was: the more handwork involved, the finer the garment.

Today, of course, this assumption isn't necessarily true. Thanks to tremendous advances in automation and technology, manufacturers are producing a more consis-tent level of quality in ready-made clothing that has been engineered to cost less. These advances have lowered cut-make-and-trim costs (the actual cost of making a gar-ment, from materials to overhead), enabling manufac-turers to buy better piecegoods (the actual textiles from which clothes are cut).

SELECTING A FABRIC   The two most important factors to consider when select-ing a suit fabric are comfort and serviceability, and you should determine your needs in these areas before mak-ing aesthetic decisions.

Where you live should influence your fabric selection in order to get long-term value. Some fabrics claim to be year-round in purpose, and if you live in, say, San Fran-cisco, where the climate is fairly mild all year, these fab-rics might make sense. But in most areas of the United States, where winters and summers are distinct and often extreme, year-round fabrics just don't offer any real degree of serviceability. You need a summer suit and a winter suit, and more than likely several of each.

Consider also where you'll wear the suit on a daily basis. If you spend most of the day in an office, which would of course be kept warm in the winter, you would be consistently uncomfortable in a heavy suit fabric; in this case a midweight fabric would make more sense. But if the summers are hot and humid where you live, even a midweight fabric would be too heavy, and you should choose from the lighter weights. Just keep in mind that lightweight fabrics, by the very nature of their lightness, must be appropriately lined for sufficient shape retention. Also, tailoring must be precise. With highly textured, or lofty, piecegoods it is easy to conceal construction flaws, but in a lightweight suit these flaws can be glaring. (More on lining and tailoring later.)

If you travel to any extent, another consideration is a garment's upkeep, or whether a fabric will require more time and expense for cleaning, pressing, and repairs than you can afford.

For many years the only kinds of fabric used in tailoring men's clothing were pure-finish fibers—all-wool, all-cotton, all-silk, etc.—and the various weaves within them: sharkskin-finished wool, tropical and mill-finished worsteds, saxonies, cheviots. Most of us still prefer these pure-finish suit fibers, simply because they are natural, or "the real thing," and because they lend a garment better breathability and more comfort in general. But they also cost more than synthetics and require more upkeep.

What about polyester? It's true that when it was first introduced in the menswear industry, it very quickly acquired a rather poor reputation. It did seem to cheapen the nature of the natural fibers it was blended with, and people just didn't take to it at all.

Back then, an all-polyester suit looked exactly like what it was: a chemical product. The double-knit suit became an albatross to the menswear industry. Not only did it look and feel chemical, but it also stretched out, snagged, and bagged.

But the advances in automation and technology helped polyester redeem itself somewhat. Manufacturers discovered that it could be spun, patterned, and woven so that it looked like wool. It gave us a garment that stayed crisp all day long and didn't stretch out, snag, or bag, and men began to change their minds about synthetic fibers in clothing.

If wearability and easy maintenance are among your prime considerations in a suit, keep in mind also the polyester *blend*. Polyester can be combined with any pure fiber, and the resulting blend is *more* desirable, in terms of upkeep and shape retention, than a pure-finish fiber. The introduction of a degree of polyester to lightweight summer fabrics such as silk and linen, which wrinkle considerably in pure finish, will help them stay crisper and neater all day. If you hang a polyblend suit on a hanger at the end of the day, what wrinkles are there will probably fall right out—an obvious advantage for the man who has to wear a suit daily.

One thing to keep in mind when buying polyester or polyester blends is that, because it is the result of a chemical process, polyester does not take color the way a natural fiber does. The higher the percentage of polyester in the blend, the more difficult it becomes to obtain certain colors. Most of the subtle deco colors cannot be adequately achieved when polyester is present in a high percentage. If you're not a "fashion purist," this probably won't matter much to you. But we do suggest that you shop carefully in any color range in order to avoid mismatching.

A quality suit must be constructed correctly. Before you even try a suit on, there are certain signs of quality work you should look for. **CONSTRUCTION AND FIT**

First, ascertain whether the manufacturer used a clothing canvas in the front of the suit jacket, between the shell fabric and the lining. A clothing canvas is used to make the jacket lie flat and mold more correctly to your body; it improves shape retention and absorbs the stress your body creates against the shell fabric, thus helping to extend the life of the garment. Since it is difficult to know for certain whether a clothing canvas was used, ask the salesperson. Ask also whether the front of the suit has a floating chestpiece. This means that fewer stitches were used when the chestpiece was set in, allowing it to float more easily over a greater portion of that area and absorb stress on the shell fabric.

Check to see whether a fusible material was used instead of a clothing canvas. As its name implies, a fusible is a material that has been melted or pressured into the front of the suit, to serve the same function as a clothing canvas, between the lining and the shell fabric. A fusible is simply a quicker and cheaper way of giving a suit its necessary shape retention.

To ascertain for yourself whether a fusible was used,

take the lapel of the jacket between your thumb and forefinger and slowly rub it back and forth. If there is an obvious stiffness, it's more than likely a fusible was used. To know for sure, however, ask.

Since fusibles are used in most ready-made suits in this country today, a discussion of their advantages and disadvantages may be academic. But there is no doubt that a fusible is not used in the best quality suits. Since a fusible is the result of a chemical process, it can break down in the dry-cleaning process. And if it wasn't set into the garment properly, dry cleaners face the additional problem of "differential shrinkage," in which the fusible shrinks to a greater extent than the shell fabric and the lining. Differential shrinkage creates a pulling and puckering effect on the jacket. Needless to say, if you come across a new suit that already has this pulling and puckering, pass it up.

Finally, take note of the lining, an important factor in how a suit will fit and wear. Was it sewn in neatly, with a measured hand? Note the stitching—the more stitches per inch, the better the garment. And as for the lining itself, you don't want too little fabric, nor do you want too much; the amount of lining fabric should correspond directly to the amount of shell fabric it rests against. (More on lining later.)

Now, having satisfied yourself that the suit meets the above requirements, check for the following construction qualities that can be determined only when you have the garment on.

The Suit Jacket How the collar on a suit jacket was made directly affects how the jacket will fit, and a well-made collar should hug

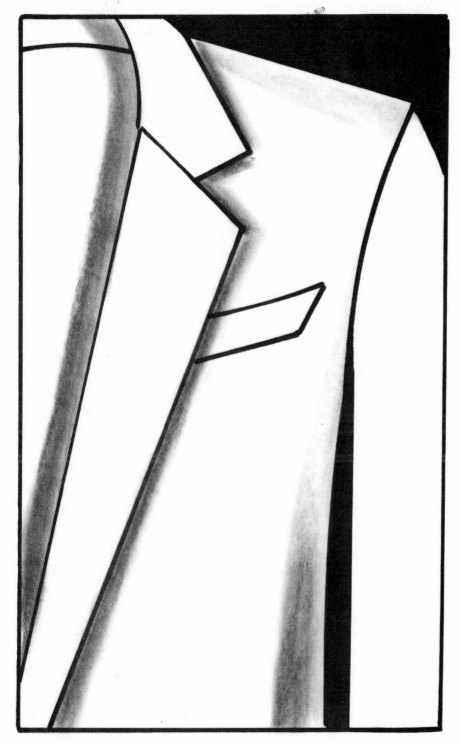

1. Collar lies smooth and naturally hugs the neck.
2. Shoulder line lies smooth.
3. Sleeve set in smoothly—no ripples or puckering.
4. Lapel lies smooth down front of jacket—no buckling across chest.

your shirt collar snugly. There should be no gaping whatsoever between the back of your shirt collar and the suit itself. If there is, either your chest or shoulder blades are pushing against the jacket in such a way that the collar is pushed back, or you've simply tried on a shoddy garment. The former problem can be solved through alteration, the latter by looking for a better garment.

Check the collar for the felling, a small piece of felt that helps give the collar pliability and shape retention.

Once you've made sure the collar rests snugly against the back of your neck, see that the lapels are lying absolutely flat against the body of the jacket, and that in the seaming of the jacket that is visible, there is no pulling or puckering as the result of faulty stitching.

Now, in front of a three-way mirror—and any good men's store should have one—take note of the shoulder area. A well-made suit jacket has a straight shoulder line. In a ready-made suit a correct shoulder fit is especially essential, because what alterations can be done in this area are very costly. Study the shoulder line carefully in the back, letting your eyes travel a straight course from the top of the collar to the edge of one shoulder, then back all the way across to the edge of the other shoulder. That line, from shoulder to shoulder, should be perfectly straight. The entire shoulder and upper back area, length and breadth, should be perfectly smooth and flat. Horizontal wrinkles mean the jacket is too tight; vertical wrinkles, that it's too full.

It's important that the shoulder also fit comfortably. A well-made suit jacket takes the elemental facts of your body's shoulder and back construction into consideration, moving with the natural motion of your body.

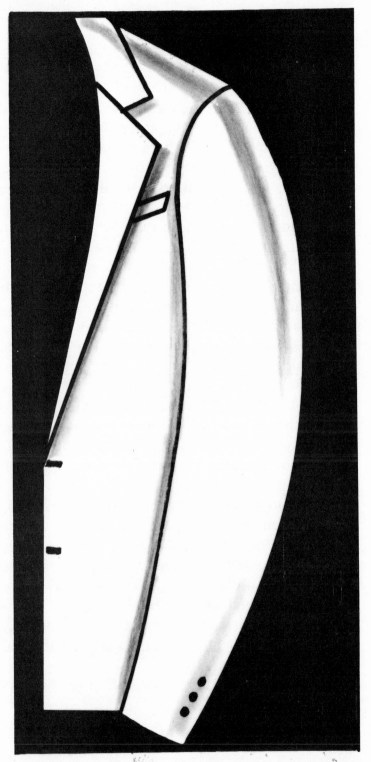

1. *Quality sleeve set in by hand—shifts slightly forward as your arm naturally does.*
2. *Tapers gently from shoulder to hem.*
3. *Make sure it's not too tight or too full.*

Now study the jacket's sleeves. The sleeve on a well-made jacket tapers *gently*, from the top of the shoulder down to where the wrist is. It should be neither tubelike nor triangular in shape, and there should never be too much space from where the wrist is to where the sleeve ends.

Sleeves, like collars, can be set in by hand or by machine, but the general consensus is that a sleeve set in by hand is better. The reason for this is that in relation to your body, the natural pitch of your arm is forward, and in building a suit to accommodate this fact, the human hand seems to understand the pitch relationship better than a machine does. A quality manufacturer understands the human body and tries to accommodate it. In this case, a sleeve set in with the human factor in mind makes for greater comfort and reduced stress on the garment. So, while the jacket is still on the hanger, note whether the sleeves are pitched slightly forward—at a human angle, so to speak. The same should hold true when you have it on. If a jacket sleeve just hangs straight down against your body, eventually you're going to develop a fold in the fabric at the back of the arm near the shoulder, which is a critical stress point to begin with.

About shoulder pads. Like many men, you may like the effect they create, but remember that they're totally a matter of style, having little to do with the quality of the garment itself. If one of your shoulders is smaller than the other, which sometimes happens, a shoulder pad can improve the fit of the jacket. Remember, though, that no alteration technique can correct a shoddily constructed shoulder on a suit.

If the suit you're considering is of a patterned fabric,

1. Pocket flaps sewn on evenly and balanced on each side.
2. Pocket under flap does not pull or sag.
3. Pocket firmly sewn inside (major stress point).

examine it carefully for pattern consistency. A manufacturer who sends out a suit whose stripes, checks, or plaids don't match has paid little attention to construction or quality control.

Plaids are especially difficult to match in a suit. Matching means that the pattern flows smoothly not only on the back center seams but also from the sleeves to the body of the jacket. In other words, when you stand up straight, the plaid should match all the way across. When you button the jacket, the front should also match perfectly, in both directions. There should be a degree of matching in the lapels. Check all the seams closely—a plaid must match there, too. And, finally, check the pants for matching as well.

If you're considering a striped suit, keep in mind that the darts that are often used in the front of a suit to enhance its shape may cause a stripe to be lost. Especially in a chalk-stripe suit, this can be a glaring flaw.

Test the buttons. On a well-made suit the buttonhole is perfectly finished, with no loose threads around it. Make sure the buttons were attached correctly, which means they were anchored securely. The button neck should be perfectly finished, with a healthy loop of thread twisted around it for additional reinforcement. If the button neck is too short (sewn too close to the fabric), the button will be difficult if not impossible to close. If the neck is too long, the effect will be of the garment "pulling away."

Years ago, suit jackets were made with buttons on the sleeves that actually opened and closed, so that a man could roll back his sleeves when he washed his hands. A nice touch, and an indication that the manufacturer cared about details. But the buttons on most jacket sleeves don't serve this practical purpose today. What's

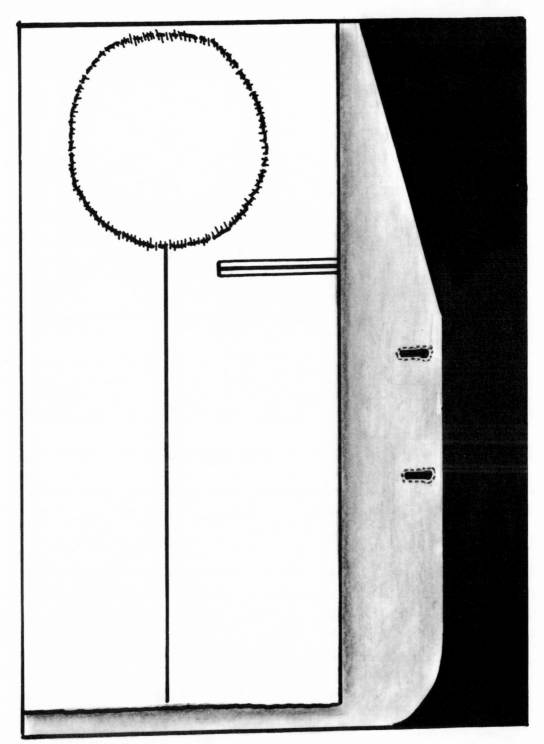

1. Best quality sleeves sewn by hand.
2. Lining even, not hanging down or loose.
3. Sewn securely.
4. Inside pocket (big stress point) large enough to accommodate wallet or pocket secretary.
5. Buttonholes tightly sewn—correct size to accommodate buttons.

important is that the buttons were put on securely and cleanly, and that when those in the front are closed, there is a perfectly flat and smooth visual effect.

The lining in a suit jacket has a direct effect on the garment's wearability and comfort. "Fully lined" means *fully lined*, collar to hem, front to back. Today, however, a three-eighths lining is standard in most suit jackets. This means that, in addition to the jacket's front lining, only three eighths of the *back* of the jacket has been lined—from the top of the collar down to just past the shoulder blades. As for the lining fabric itself, a well-made jacket is usually lined with Bemberg rayon, soft and silky to the touch, with excellent shape-retention qualities and "dry-cleanability." The tag in the back of the jacket should tell you whether Bemberg rayon was used; if not, ask.

To say that a suit jacket without a lining is inferior would not be entirely correct. Unlined, or "unconstructed," garments began when designers chose to approach tailored clothing with a bit more relaxed and sporty attitude, taking the "tailored" feeling out of the boardroom, so to speak, and onto the boardwalk. They redefined the tailored garment, changing it from a piece of "armor" into an element of dress more fully integrated into one's total lifestyle. Stylistically, the unconstructed suit jacket has evolved into a popular statement. What you must keep in mind, however, is that the basic European garment was so beautifully made that the lack of lining did not cheapen it. If you decide on an unlined suit jacket, make certain the seams are taped (a technique in which a tape is sewn over the ragged edges of the unfinished seams to give them a cleaner appearance), and that the jacket as a whole has been well constructed.

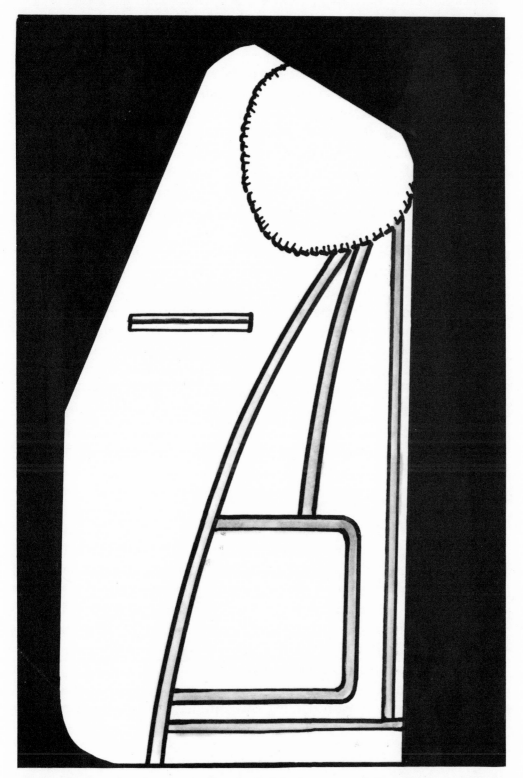

1. *Unconstructed suit—seams cleanly finished, no ragged threads.*
2. *When garment is on it should look as smooth as a fully constructed suit.*

Now, once you have determined that the suit jacket you're considering was properly constructed, and that it fits you as accurately as possible, consider whether it gives your body a definite shape. The "drop" of a suit is the amount of difference between the chest measurement of the jacket and the waist measurement of the trouser. For many years, most American suits were made with what is referred to as a 6-inch drop, which meant that a size 40 jacket always came with a 34-inch-waist trouser. However, since the late sixties, and through the seventies, the 7-inch-drop suit has become widely popular.

Your choice between the 6-inch and 7-inch drop will be mostly a matter of style, but your body type has a lot to do with it. Since the 7-inch-drop suit is designed with the more physique-oriented man in mind, and since the 7-inch-drop pattern is actually cut closer to the body, with less bulk of fabric, it needs a trim figure to look right. If your figure is other than trim, a 7-inch-drop suit is not going to represent quality from two standpoints: It won't look right on you, and because it doesn't fit properly, it just won't last.

The Suit Pant

A suit pant's basic elements of quality, in both construction and fit, must live up to those of the jacket, or the unit simply doesn't work. Let's study the standard suit pant as a separate (but equal) component.

In many ways the lining, and how it was put in, is more important to the proper construction of the pant than it is to that of the jacket. A man creates more stress on a pair of pants than he does on a jacket. A suit jacket can be removed over the course of a day, reducing the amount of stress it would have to contend with if you were constantly moving in it. Most of us keep our trousers on, however, and we're constantly bending, turning, and twisting in them; we carry change, keys, wallets, and even our hands in the pockets, which creates additional stress. Add to this the punishment we give the knees when we stoop, squat, or even just sit (and the seat of the pant sees its share of stress too), and the importance of a pant lining is obvious.

A well-constructed suit pant should have a high-quality cotton lining in the waistband and the pockets. Check also whether the pant has a crotchpiece, a lining fabric, often of the same material as the rest of the pant lining, that covers the area where the inner thighs meet. The crotchpiece acts as a stress absorber, to protect the shell fabric from the constant rubbing together of the thighs, and, conversely, adds comfort by protecting the skin from possible irritation by the fabric.

The crotch of a pant is a major stress point, and a quality manufacturer will probably have added the crotchpiece. However, the lack of a crotchpiece does not necessarily imply shoddy construction. An all-polyester suit, for instance, really doesn't require one, because of the nature of the fabric. Simply keep in mind that a crotchpiece never detracts from the quality of a suit, and its presence will at least tell you that the manufacturer cared enough to add it.

Similarly, not all pant legs are lined, depending on the fabric, its personality, drapability, etc. A texturized polyester pant, for example, doesn't require a lining in the leg, for the same reasons it doesn't require a crotchpiece. On the other hand, a Donegal tweed suit (without a lining) is cheap. If pant legs are lined, whether a lining was called for or not, so much the better.

The lining in a pant leg can be of either nylon or Bemberg rayon; a cheaper fabric you may encounter is poly/rayon. Rub the lining back and forth between your fingers: If it's thin and slick, it's probably a cheaper lining. Though Bemberg is the finer-quality lining material—because of its excellent shape retention and dry-cleanability—there's nothing intrinsically *wrong* with a cheaper lining; just remember that that is what you should be paying for—a cheaper lining. By the way, there is no reason why a pant must be lined much past the knee, since most men wear over-the-calf socks anyway. Excess can detract from quality as much as a sore lack can; why have to pay for something that isn't needed? A quality manufacturer gives you exactly what you need—no more, no less.

Avoid lighter-weight summer suits, especially in white or lighter summer shades, that aren't adequately lined. The lining will solve the problem of show-through and enhance shape retention—particularly important on hot, muggy days. A beige or white lightweight summer suit, say in a silk or linen blend, just won't wear or look right if it hasn't been lined adequately.

In sum, the lining of a suit pant should be one of your foremost criteria when judging a suit's construction. Make sure it's neither skimpy nor overabundant, and that it was put in properly—no loose threads, and an ample amount of stitches used to put it in (remember, the more stitches per inch, the better).

A quality suit pant will always have what is known as a fully constructed waistband. This means that a piece of clothing canvas has been inserted between the shell fabric of the waistband and its lining, to give the waistband shape retention and to reduce the amount of stress and strain on the shell fabric itself. The clothing canvas reinforces the shell fabric and keeps it standing up straight at all times, whether you're wearing a belt or not. Though there is really no way (aside from slitting it open) to tell if the waistband was fully constructed or not, you should use your fingers to test the band for strength and pliability just as you did the lapel of the jacket. You should also ask.

Now consider the fit, also a function of how the pant was constructed. The waistband should, of course, fit your girth comfortably, and should stand up straight, with no curl-over whatsoever, whether you're wearing a belt or not. Incidentally, it is unimportant in terms of construction quality whether a suit pant has belt loops or not. That's purely a matter of style.

The rise of the pant—the area from the bottom of the zipper to the top of the pant—should fit you snugly but comfortably. Naturally, you don't want the crotch to be down past your knees, nor for the obvious reasons do you want it to be too high. Keep in mind that the rise on some suit pants is deliberately cut low—again, purely a matter of style.

How the zipper was set in is another key to whether the pant was constructed with any degree of quality, and to whether it will fit you right. Sometimes the zipper is sewn in too tightly, resulting in a rippling effect along the fly. A pulling effect near the top of the pant, from the top of the zipper to where the pant buttons, is also an indication of shoddy construction.

As to which is the better zipper, plastic or metal, the answer is mostly academic. Plastic costs less to replace and doesn't rust; but since plastic is the result of a chemical process, it can break down or weaken in the drycleaning process. Metal, of course, is stronger than plastic. Your choice will have to be based on what you prefer, and what the manufacturer has seen fit to offer—a great many suit pants today have plastic zippers.

Now use the three-way mirror to make certain the pants fit correctly in the thigh area. This means that even if the pant is pleated, the fabric should encompass your thighs without so much as a wrinkle, ripple, or pucker to distort its natural, smooth line. Unless you're a runner, with highly developed thighs and calves (something you'll have to take into consideration, and live with, when you shop for clothing), a suit pant was not constructed correctly or isn't fitting properly if the thigh area isn't perfectly smooth—all around, front and back.

The pockets of the suit pant are another crucial area. Pockets that are too large or roomy just aren't necessary and can be uncomfortable to use; pockets that are too small will create not only additional stress on the garment but also a pulling effect in the line of the leg. When you have a suit pant on, the pocket should lie absolutely flat, and there should be no bulging, pulling, or gaping. On the inside of the pocket there should also be enough of the suit fabric to cover the opening; you should never see the lining of a pocket.

Pockets are meant to serve a strictly functional purpose—to put things in—and a quality manufacturer will have attended to this purpose through proper construction. A pocket must be strong, well lined (in 100%, high-quality cotton), and strongly stitched.

We advise carrying as little as possible in the pockets

1. *Collar hugs neck and lies flat.*
2. *Lapel lies flat—edges do not curl.*
3. *Shoulder line perfectly smooth.*
4. *Sleeve set in smoothly—no puckers.*
5. *Buttons securely anchored.*
6. *Cleanly sewn buttonholes.*
7. *Pockets set evenly on each side.*
8. *Front of jacket lies perfectly smooth when buttoned—no ripples or X effect.*
9. *Chest lies smoothly on body without pulling.*

of your suit pant, simply because this will reduce the stress the pant must deal with over an extended period of time. If you wear a suit every day and own three, slipping your wallet into the back pocket on a daily basis will stretch out the fabric and ultimately take its toll on the garment in much less time than it should. Why not try carrying your wallet in your jacket pocket?

TAILORING
AND
MAINTENANCE

Once you have established that a suit was constructed correctly, it may require alteration to fit you more properly. Tailoring is the responsibility of the store you're buying the suit from, and we urge you not to be content with having only the sleeves and cuffs attended to if the suit requires more work to make it fit right.

Regardless of the price of the suit, insist that a fitter, not a salesperson, do the measurements for tailoring. In most cases a salesperson has neither the skill nor the time to alter a suit properly, whereas a fitter's sole job is to fit or alter garments. If a salesperson does do the tailoring, keep in mind that *that* is what you should be paying for: the services of a salesperson, and not a skilled fitter.

Specialty men's stores are best equipped to handle alteration work, simply because all they ever alter is men's clothing. Their staff is geared to meet this need. On the other hand, a discount store, understandably, offers no amenities. Remember that if you get a substantial enough discount on the garment, you can probably afford to take it elsewhere for alteration.

Once you've bought a suit, if it doesn't afford you the level of quality you were led to believe you were paying for—if it comes back from the dry cleaner puckered or pulling, with loose buttons or dangling threads, with the seams coming apart or the stitching breaking down—*take it back and demand a refund*. Keep in mind that a store will often blame the dry cleaner, when in the majority of cases the dry cleaner is not at fault. A reputable dry cleaner knows better than anyone how to clean a suit properly.

As to how often you should have a suit cleaned, it's mostly a matter of need and budget. From the advice we've gotten from experts in the field, frequent dry cleaning can actually enhance the life of a garment. The biggest culprits are dirt and grime, which, when allowed to accumulate over a period of time, can wear down the fabric and diminish its visual personality.

Establish a close and personal relationship with your cleaners, and *ask* about maintenance. This is their field and their specialty, and most are extremely amenable to talking about what they know if they take any pride in what they do.

2. Tailored Sportswear

THERE should be no difference, in terms of construction quality, between a well-made sportcoat and a well-made suit jacket. In sportcoats, however, there is much greater flexibility in fabric, which affects whether some elements of construction are necessary or even appropriate.

SPORTCOATS

There is a trend in sportcoat manufacturing today toward doing less construction in "better" fabrics—"better" meaning more pure finish, meaning more expensive. Thus the consumer is offered more *perceived* value (in terms of the fabric), but less *actual* value (in terms of the garment's construction). The reasoning behind this practice is that for many men, a sportcoat is not as serious an investment as a suit. By saving on cut-make-and-trim costs, the manufacturer can offer a more expensive fabric,

Piecegoods: Perceived Value vs. Actual Value

41

which will be reflected on the garment's price tag. The *perceived* value is greater, but if the garment needed those missing construction elements to work right or simply to last, there is little *actual* value.

There *is* a smart compromise if you want a sportcoat that will both look good (perceived) and work right (actual). Let's say you want the look of Harris tweed, without the cost. The answer is a blend. It is often possible today for a manufacturer to use blended fabrics in such a way that it is very difficult to tell them from pure-finish fabrics. This is especially true of winterweight fabrics, which, because of their heaviness, can hold more polyester and are given even better shape retention by its addition. A Shetland-look sportcoat, for example, even in a blend of 60% polyester and 40% wool, will have the visual effect of pure-finish *and* the construction advantages of excellent shape retention and less wrinkling. The added bonus is that the sportcoat will cost less. From the standpoint of perceived and actual value, then, it really does make sense to buy garments that have better construction (where it's needed) in *blended fabrics*.

Getting the Quality You Need— No Less, No More

Note again that we said "where it's needed." Let's see now how the nature of the piecegoods themselves can dictate the amount of construction that should go into a quality sportcoat.

Sportcoat piecegoods weights, because of the great variety to be found in sportcoats themselves, vary a great deal more than the piecegoods offered in tailored suits. For example, you could find a cashmere sportcoat, but not a cashmere suit (unless you chose to have one made for yourself). Nor would you ever find a Harris tweed suit, while Harris tweed is rather standard in sportcoats. There are also some very lightweight—almost shirting weight—piecegoods that could be effectively used for a summer sportcoat but would be impractical for a suit.

Summerweight piecegoods can be as light as 7 ounces per yard; winterweight fabrics, as heavy as 14 ounces. All of these various weights of fabric must be constructed on the same machinery in the clothing plant, and it stands to reason that each reacts in a different way. A needle and thread goes through a 14-ounce topcoat-weight wool differently than through a 7-ounce all-cotton fabric. Each fabric requires different construction elements in order to work right in the garment's final shape.

Here's the rule of thumb for a winterweight sportcoat: If you are going to wear it as a "dressy" garment, for business and other more formal settings, you should look for the same elements of quality construction you would look for in a suit jacket. If, however, you intend to wear a winterweight sportcoat more as an item of sportswear— as a "play" coat—then your quality standards can be relaxed somewhat, since the heavier fabric's natural drapability and lofty surface require less construction and will even, as we've mentioned, hide some construction flaws.

Summerweight sportcoat fabrics are another matter entirely. Because they are by nature lighter and not as lofty as winterweight fabrics, hiding construction flaws is more difficult. In effect, then, construction quality in summerweight sportcoats must be *better* than it is in winterweights. Most summerweight fabrics have less inherent drapability and shape retention to begin with, and a good deal of construction is needed to give them these qualities. For this reason, you should not expect a price differential between summer- and winterweight garments; construction costs will be greater in a well-made lightweight garment because of the linings, padding, or whatever is needed to give the garment greater shape retention and drapability.

Like a winterweight sportcoat, a summerweight sportcoat that you intend to wear for sport or play does not really need the attention to construction that dressier coats do. We have no objection to elements of construction quality existing where they aren't really needed—but why pay for something you don't need? In a casual summerweight sportcoat, you really shouldn't be looking for such construction elements as canvas, fusing, or felling under the collar.

However, if you're buying a summerweight sportcoat that will serve as a dress garment, proper construction is everything; you should look for all the standard elements of quality construction you would look for in a suit jacket—and more.

Because summer in the United States is hot and humid in most areas, a proper *lining* in a dressy summerweight sportcoat is crucial not only to the garment's working right, but also to its overall wearability and lifespan. A lining will help keep a summerweight sportcoat crisp and unwrinkled throughout the day, and enhance the garment's shape retention.

Also for protection, we highly recommend *armshields* in a dressy summer sportcoat. We'll even go as far as to say that if you buy a summer sportcoat without armshields, have them put in. They'll probably cost you extra, but they'll save you more in the long run by extending the life of the garment.

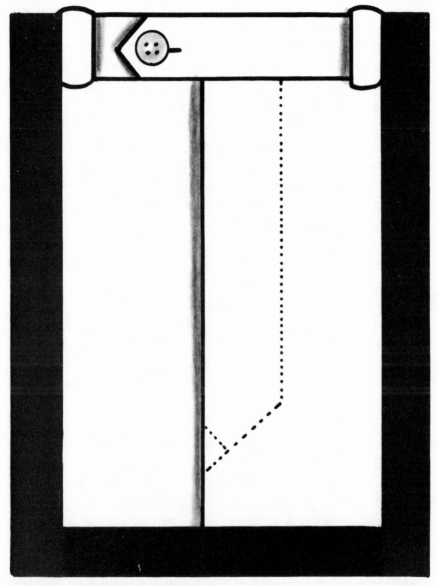

1. Smooth closure at waistband—no pulling.
2. Inside (not shown): metal closure in additon to button closure.
3. Fly lies smooth—no puckering of pulling.
4. Reinforcement at bottom of fly.

TAILORED SLACKS For many years in the men's tailored clothing industry, dress-constructed trousers that went with a sportcoat were clearly differentiated from *casual* slacks by the very nature of their construction. In fact, a dress trouser was the *only* trouser one wore with a sportcoat. The fabric may have been all-silk, all-wool, or even a blend of polyester and wool—but it was very definitely a dress pant, and you were able to tell distinctly the difference between it and a casual pant. There was simply no flexibility in what pant was worn with a sportcoat; a clear line of demarcation was drawn between the two types of pants because of their construction, and there was no overlap.

Today, however, the range of fabrics that can be used in making a pair of dress pants is much wider, from the traditional dress-pant fabrics, such as tropical-weight wool and the poly/wool blend, to the number-one-selling fabric in this country today, texturized polyester.

Elements of Quality Construction A tailored pant in its purest form should be as well made as suit pants. It should have a fully constructed waistband, a zipper that has been set in correctly, pockets that work properly—all of the standard elements of construction quality you would demand in a good suit pant.

In a well-made pair of dress slacks, look also for what is known as a French fly, an extra piece of fabric sewn into the right side of the pant and extending to the left side, where it buttons. This helps provide the front of the pant with a smoother fit, and affords additional support in a primary area of stress.

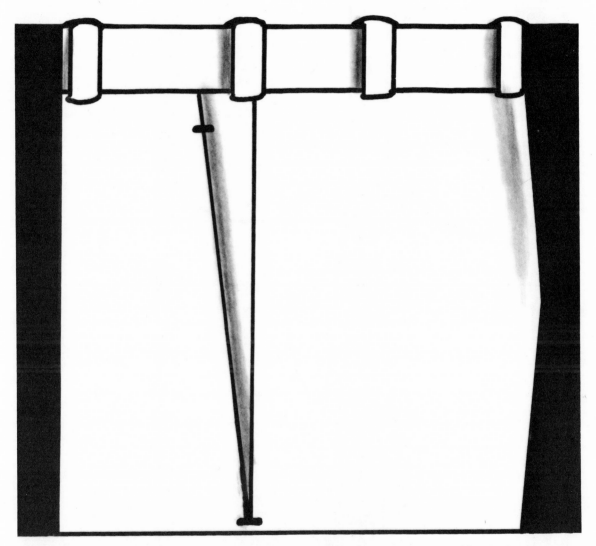

1. Belt loops turned and sewn under, giving smooth appearance—no visible stitching.
2. Firmly constructed waistline with no curlover at top.
3. Pockets bar-tacked at top and bottom—major stress points.
4. Pocket opening large enough to easily accommodate hand.
5. Pant seams evenly sewn—no puckers.

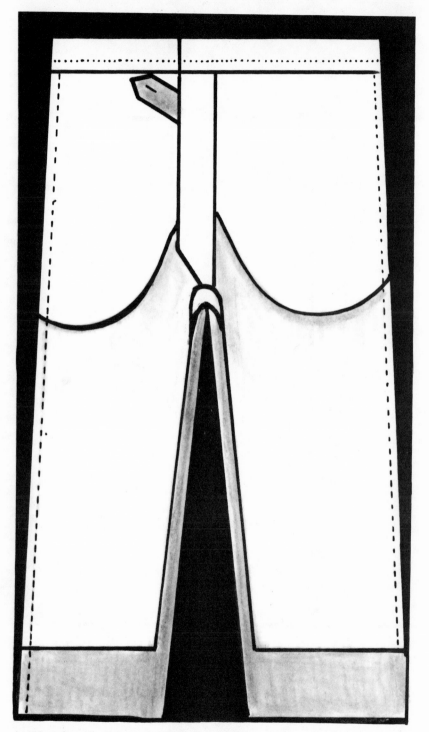

1. *Waistband and pocket lining of high-quality cotton—carefully and neatly sewn.*
2. *Pant leg lining fits inside of leg appropriately—make sure you can move comfortably.*
3. *Lining should end at knee.*
4. *Inside of fly should be lined.*
5. *Crotchpiece and inside button closure (French fly)—quality touches.*

As for a lining in a dress pant, you should have one if the fabric is highly textured, to prevent irritation of the skin and the fabric wearing itself out by rubbing together, and because it absorbs stress, thus preventing the fabric from stretching out. Keep in mind, though, that some fabrics don't require a lining. Such fabrics as cavalry twill, some lightweight worsted wools, and gabardine weaves have better shape retention and wearability, and because of their smooth finish, they do not have that problem of rubbing together and pilling between the thighs. For these reasons, these and other hardy, smooth-finish fabrics simply do not require a lining in a pant. Again, why pay more—and a lining can cost you *a lot* more—for something you don't need?

Many summerweight fabrics require a lining, either because they do not have the natural drapability, shape retention, and wearability of the winterweights, or because their light color allows "show-through." There's nothing tackier than having your pocket linings or your underwear show through a summer garment.

To sum up: define the end use of the garment you're buying and adjust your quality standards to meet it. Impracticality is not quality, and paying for unnecessary quality isn't value. Unlike tailored suits, tailored sportswear ranges widely in its levels of quality. Be flexible, suiting the garment to its role in your lifestyle, and your clothing dollars will go a long, long way.

3. Shirts

THOUGH it probably isn't news in today's inflated economic climate, the price of men's shirting has skyrocketed in the last few years. Couple this with the fact that men are being offered a wider selection of colors and patterns that are acceptable as standard dress wear, and we have a segment of the menswear market that requires an especially acute shopping awareness.

At the bottom line, the key issue in building any wardrobe should always be one of getting the most value for the money being spent. Building a dress-shirt wardrobe is no exception to this rule, and for several reasons—some obvious, some not so obvious—it requires an even stronger adherence to it. For example, most men purchase dress shirts with an existing wardrobe in mind. Logical questions when doing this are: Will this pattern work with my herringbone jacket? Will it work equally well with my pinstripe? Will this color work as well with one suit as with another? Although we haven't entirely retired the dependable white shirt and safe dark tie as a standard business image, it simply isn't the *only* image anymore, and so these questions about coordination have become increasingly important.

These questions, however, are secondary to that of the shirt's construction quality, without which versatility is of no value.

A well-made shirt is always a value, regardless of its cost. Good construction increases a shirt's lifespan, and once you know what to look for when buying, problems of color and pattern coordination can be properly dealt with.

THE WELL-MADE DRESS SHIRT: KEY CONSTRUCTION COMPONENTS

When you're shopping for a dress shirt with an eye toward quality in construction, two key features—the collar and the stitching—will reveal a lot about the overall work that went into making the garment. Other components and subcomponents of the shirt's construction will bear out what these two primary components have told you.

The Collar

The standard dress shirt collar will be constructed in one of two ways. One way, found in better-quality dress shirts, is with an inner facing—a separate fabric insert—between the two pieces of collar fabric, which gives the collar softness while maintaining its shape-retention ability. The other way is with a fused collar lining, a lining that is permanently fused to the collar's outer layer, also enabling the collar to lie flatter and neater, and retain its shape.

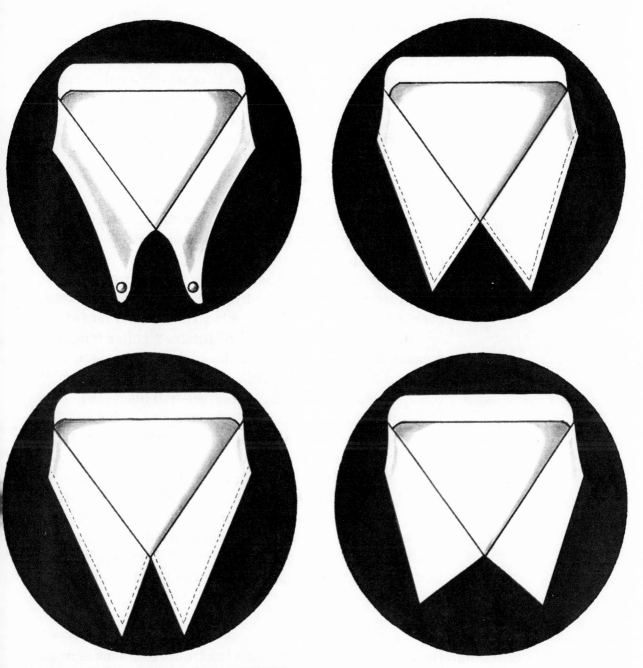

FOUR COLLAR STYLES: COMMON CHARACTERISTICS

1. *Look for even construction—make sure sides are balanced.*
2. *Collar should fit snugly around neck.*
3. *Tight, even stitching with no puckering, or firm fusing with no puckering.*
4. *Make sure shirt collar can accommodate neckwear knot, and that back of collar is high enough to cover neckband of tie.*

One other collar construction feature that can indicate care and attention to tailoring is removable collar stays. The purpose of a collar stay is to keep the collar lying flat and straight. Removable stays are better than permanent stays, which, if broken, will leave the collar permanently bent.

The collar cape—the collar's outer edge—will be either straight or scooped (curved) in shape, and will be available in several standard proportions (see illustration). The alternative button-down collar is also available in these proportions.

In terms of fashion, the collar is the feature of a shirt that is most apt to change from season to season. Whatever is happening to suit lapels will have a direct effect on collar lengths. As a note of interest, collar length is measured from the point of the collar to the seam it is attached to. Further, the collar of a shirt plays an integral role in overall shirt sizing, which we will discuss shortly. It is important to select a shirt with a collar that is wide enough to permit the wearing of a tie with any size knot. Keep in mind also that most shirts are packaged in a way that does not allow thorough inspection of the collar, so do not be afraid to remove it for examination. Finally, a brand-new shirt has been pressed by a professional presser, so that any pucker that appears after the fabric is washed was probably always there. If the collar doesn't lie right after washing, it's not your fault—*take it back to the store!*

Stitching How a shirt has been stitched is a true, visible measure of its quality. Remember, it's the thread that holds the garment together. The more stitches per inch, the stronger the shirt and the more attention has been paid to its construction. A shirt with 22 stitches per inch is a well-constructed shirt.

Hastily constructed shirts tell on themselves—pulled stitching or a loose thread where the machine finished its job is indisputable evidence of sloppy work. And, once again, if a pucker has been stitched in, your iron can't correct it; it'll only worsen, affecting the overall quality of the shirt, and you should return this defective garment to the store.

Today, shirt manufacturers use two basic stitching techniques: single-needle or double-needle. This means that the shirt was stitched together on a machine equipped with either one or two needles. The logical question is, does it really matter, in terms of quality, which technique was used in stitching a shirt together? The answer is yes, and here's why.

Contrary to what you might think, two needles are not better than one when a shirt is being stitched at the seams. The double-needle process puts the shirt fabric through a high-speed machine, and although this may indeed put a shirt together very quickly, it does not ensure that it will be put together as well as it would be in the single-needle process. For example, the manner in which the sleeves are set into the shoulder of a shirt is crucial to the final fit of the shirt: the sleeves must be stitched into the shoulders all the way around, front and back, and with the double-needle machine moving so rapidly it becomes difficult to control the consistency of the stitching. What you can end up with is ripples and a pulling effect along the sides of the shirt body because the sleeves were stitched in sloppily.

Single-needle stitching is done on a different kind of

machine, which is easier to control. Also, the double-needle machine stitches the entire shirt together, shoulder and body seams, in one uninterrupted step, whereas the single-needle machine requires two steps: the machine stitches one side of the seam from beginning to end, is stopped, and then the other side of the seam is stitched. Thus, it is a slower, more controlled—and of course costlier—technique. The result is stronger, more durable stitching. On top of this, single-needle stitching is also more aesthetically pleasing, because you will not see the stitches. What the manufacturer does is take the seam on the outside and turn it under, hiding the stitches from the eye. It's simply neater, and nicer to look at. It's also the best way to know whether a shirt was single- or double-needle stitched or not, if the label doesn't tell you (though most will, because the maker is proud of it).

Most shirts today are double-needle stitched, though you will find some that are single-needle stitched at the shoulder and double-needle stitched along the body seams. Single-needle stitching is definitely a sign of quality, and it will cost you more. But be aware that you should be paying less for a shirt that was both single- and double-needle stitched than you should for one that was completely single-needle stitched, and even less for one that was completely double-needle stitched.

Plackets and Button Treatments   Look for a full sleeve placket with a button, an indication of quality in construction because it causes the cuff to lie a little flatter. A full-placket front also indicates greater attention to construction detail; choose the shirt with the wider placket, as it will give the front of the shirt a neater look. (Keep in mind, though, that there is also the French front shirt—the front is simply flat, without a placket. This, too, can be a well-constructed garment, though it is usually sportier, as a French front is easier to use when matching fabric patterns.)

Yet another means of determining how well a shirt was constructed is from its buttons and buttonholes. First, look for mother-of-pearl buttons, since most are plastic. More important, however, is how the buttons have been attached to the shirt, and how their corresponding buttonholes were put in. Shirt buttons, as well as their holes, are put in by machines. Often the section of the plant responsible for putting on the buttons is separate from the section where the holes are put in. If one button is off-center in relation to its corresponding hole, it will create an overall disruptive effect on the body of the shirt, causing an excess fabric fold. Watch for this.

Fabric

Once you have satisfied yourself as to the shirt's construction, the fabric from which the shirt has been cut becomes a primary consideration. As there are only two basic dress-shirt fabrics, your decision here will not be a complicated one. But you should know the facts about each fabric.

For the most part, better-quality shirts are produced from 100% cotton. Cotton tends to dye better, so that it is possible to achieve a wide range of subtle colors, and most people agree that cotton is more comfortable to wear. All-cotton fabric also absorbs body moisture, rather than trapping it between the shirt and the wearer, and thus can be said to "breathe" better.

On the minus side, cotton requires greater maintenance because it wrinkles easily. A shirt constructed of 100% cotton, though apt to be well made, will not travel well.

Polyester, on the other hand, requires minimal maintenance, but its absorption qualities are nil. The result is a shirt that can be sticky, clingy, and plain uncomfortable in warm weather.

Poly/cotton blends—the most common being 65% poly/35% cotton—seem to have found the neutral ground between these two fabrics, marrying the best qualities of both in one shirt. Most popular-priced dress shirts are constructed of this particular poly-cotton blend, though of late "reverse blends" (40% poly/60% cotton) have come close to matching the finish and the comfort properties of 100% cotton. On the whole, when you have a choice between 100% cotton or a poly/cotton blend in a dress shirt, the better value is really the one that ultimately meets your greatest need. The deciding factor is in caring for the garment itself, based on which you have more of—time or money.

Whichever fiber content you settle on, the fabric itself will have been woven in one of three standard weaves. *Broadcloth*, because of its tight weave and smooth finish, is the most formal weave, and the predominant choice for constructing dressier shirts. *End-and-end* weaves have a somewhat less smooth finish, and tend to have a slightly more casual attitude about them. The classic use of *Oxford* cloth is in button-down-collar shirts, though it certainly isn't limited to this style.

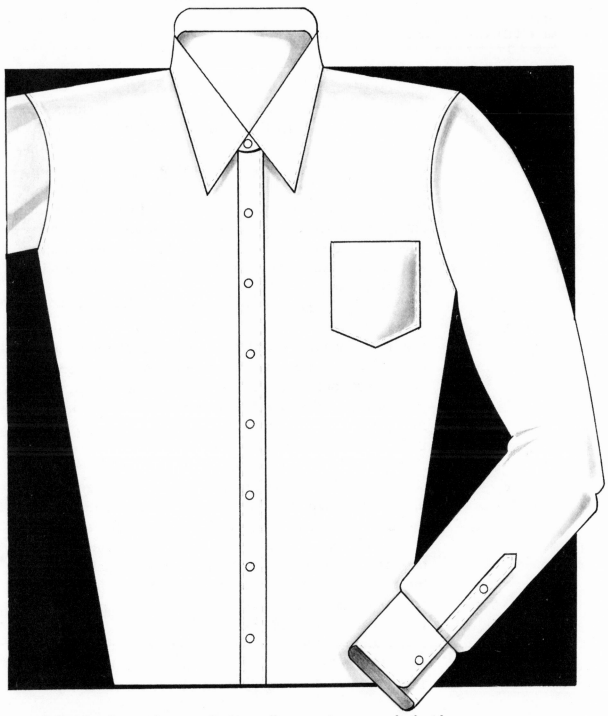

1. Collar lies flat, with no puckering; collar cape is even on both sides.
2. Placket—either full placket or French front—should lie flat.
3. Buttons firmly anchored and of good quality.
4. Pocket sewn on evenly.
5. Sleeve placket with button—an added quality touch.

Sizing Today, there two common fits in men's dress shirts: the standard cut and the fitted cut. The fitted shirt is European in origin, and is designed to fit the contours of the body closely—a tailoring preference of European men. European and American men's body types differ to the point that American manufacturers had to translate this cut into American terms; they introduced a trimming effect in the chest and body by cutting the pattern smaller and adding back darts. The fitted shirt also has a slimmer-fitting sleeve.

The factor to keep in mind when deciding whether to buy a fitted or a standard-cut shirt is your build. If yours is a trim physique, the fitted shirt may be the perfect cut. On the other hand, if your physique needs a bit of work, and you're looking to play *down* any excess bulk, you'll probably want to go with the standard cut. Just keep in mind that a shirt with a darted back will follow your body's contours, whatever they may be.

When you are ready to size the shirt you have selected, check its tag for two numbers. A shirt that is sized 15/33 has a collar size of 15 inches and a sleeve length of 33 inches. You can ascertain your collar size by measuring your neck with a tape measure, slipping one finger in between. Sleeve length is arrived at by placing the tape at the center of the back of your neck and measuring across your shoulder and all the way down your arm, ending where your wrist and your hand meet.

A sizing system you may encounter is the "average shirt length." For example, a shirt might be labeled 15/32-33, which means that the sleeve length is adjustable and can be worn at 32 or 33. The cuff will have two buttons, side by side; the shorter length can be attained by buttoning the sleeve narrower, or wider for the longer length.

Now that you are able to recognize a quality-constructed shirt, you can make pattern and color selections, a knowledge of which can expand the versatility of your wardrobe.

COORDINATING THE STANDARD DRESS SHIRT: COLORS AND PATTERNS

As we mentioned earlier, most men shop for a dress shirt with a particular suit in mind. Thus it stands to reason that the more suits you can wear the shirt with, the greater value the shirt has. By maximizing a garment's versatility, you can minimize the possibility of repetition. Careful shopping will also eliminate the unnecessary expense of duplication and waste. Needless to say, there is no value in having a closet full of garments that never seem to get worn.

Standard Dress-Shirt Colors

Today's wider flexibility in color and pattern selection for a standard dress shirt has certainly not made the dependable white shirt obsolete. Because of its absolute neutrality, the standard white dress shirt presents no coordination problems whatsoever, and having a few in your wardrobe is always a good investment. Make one of them a standard French-cuff model, and you will have the option of wearing it for business or, with proper accessorization, in most dressy situations.

Another wardrobe staple is the solid-color dress shirt. Its absence of pattern makes it easy to coordinate, eliminating the problem of possible competition with a tie or a suit pattern. Certain color tones complement a man's complexion without being heavily tinted; maize yellow, pale blue, and tan are the three primary pastels used in mens' shirting. These colors will almost always be serviceable with any standard suit color. Avoid a maize when it is too lemon-colored, or a tan that is too gray, subtle variations that will nonetheless diminish a shirt's versatility.

The common secondary pastels used for men's shirting are not as easily coordinated as the primary pastels, but still have become common colors for standard dress-shirt wear over the past few years. These are ecru (a creamy beige), light gray, apricot, mint green, and pale pink. Darker dress-shirt colors are available, but they resist being called "standard" because they fall more understandably into the "fashion color" area.

Keep in mind that medium to dark tones represent the least value in terms of building a standard dress-shirt base. To get the most for your money, build your dress-shirt wardrobe in this order: white shirts first, then the primary pastels, and finally the secondary pastels. Then, if you wish, you may supplement with the darker fashion colors. You may also wish to acquire a solid pastel shirt with a white collar and cuffs, which isn't always "in fashion" but is a standard, serviceable item nonetheless.

Selecting a Functional Dress-Shirt Pattern There are several classic-patterned dress-shirt fabrics. The safest way to approach the color combinations that exist in them is to look for a consistency in *tone*—which is to say, one color should not override another.

Vertical stripes are a classic look that always works well as a primary base for a dress-shirt wardrobe. The most versatile vertical striping scheme is thin and evenly spaced. Other possibilities, which work best in softer shades, are cluster stripes, in which three or more stripes that are the same or differently colored have been clustered together; awning stripes, like the stripe often seen on awnings—a wider width, and bolder; hairline stripes, narrow and widely spaced.

Checks and plaids offer even more versatility—if selected carefully. Both tend to be too sporty for dress wear, though there are exceptions. For example, a small, monotoned tattersall or a gingham check might be worn with a herringbone jacket and a club tie.

Plaids can be more difficult to coordinate, because the shirt becomes the focal point of the ensemble. Make sure it matches in the front and is perfectly centered. An easy clue to a sloppily constructed plaid shirt is a pocket that doesn't match the body of the shirt. If this is the case, don't buy it; chances are it's a cheap shirt in other ways as well.

SHOPPING FOR SHIRTS

Here are a few basic shopping hints to further polish your expertise. First, know when a bargain is really a bargain. Merchandising is an art, and a knowledge of retailing devices will help you find that bargain and avoid the "lure."

Beware store-brand articles that are marked "On Sale." It may mean simply that the price of the article has been marked up very high for a very short amount of time, then drastically "discounted."

Let's say a store buys a shirt for $5. Ordinarily the markup would be about $10, or the traditional doubling of the original cost. Some stores, however, will mark up the shirt to $20. Legally, this shirt, marked down to $10, is a sale item. It has been discounted 50%. But it's still a $10 shirt. The "lure" is the supposed discount.

Comparison-shop on brand names, as this will give you some insight into the normal market. Stores often buy at reduced prices styles that originally, for any of a number of reasons, didn't sell well at wholesale. These items then become big "sale" articles. There must have been a reason why they didn't sell well in the first place. Inquire of a salesperson whether the garment on sale was ordered especially for sale stock. Most will answer honestly, but if there is any doubt, think twice.

We'll now offer you one of the best bargain tips available: Currently, shirts made in Hong Kong are an excellent value. Because labor costs are lower in Hong Kong than in the U.S. or Europe, the products Hong Kong offers are a great deal less expensive, but there is usually no compromise in quality. Do not be put off by a Hong Kong label. You'll be buying quality without the sting of paying excessively for it.

4. Neckties

No other item in your wardrobe says "you" as clearly as a necktie does. It allows you to move beyond the normal constraints of taste that suits and shirts must conform to, and is in fact the article of clothing that invites the most creative expression.

In the menswear industry, an article of neckwear is frequently referred to as a "blind item," which means it is difficult to ascertain the true value of a tie, as opposed to the price it is offered at. Who's to say why a specific tie is priced at $28.50, $22.50, $18.50, or $12.50? What are the criteria, and whose are they? Quite often, a consumer will be offered a tie that is simply expensive, but hasn't been constructed well at all. It's just a tie that's expensive, and that's all. The color may be beautiful, the pattern stunning—but these are *perceived* values. To have actual value, to be worth the money you're paying for, a tie must have been constructed properly.

CONSTRUCTION The amount of construction that goes into a necktie varies according to the fabric used to make the tie. As we've seen, some fabrics need more construction attention than others, and so various levels of tie construction are acceptable. No tie, however, should be totally unconstructed. Unlike many other items in your wardrobe, a tie undergoes a tremendous amount of intentionally applied stress. You're tying that tie in a knot, after all.

We feel that there are basic elements of construction that should be present in a quality tie, regardless of the fabric.

The first of these is an inner facing. Much like the clothing canvas in a suit jacket, it helps the tie retain its shape, and is also a stress absorber. It is cut in the shape of the tie itself and attached at either end to the shell fabric.

Without actually slitting the tie open, it's difficult to know whether the inner facing has been put in. You may wish to test by "feel," taking the tie at the larger end between the fingers and thumbs of both hands and, very gently so as not to damage it, pulling the back of the tie away from the outer shell. What should be left, between the two pieces of fabric, is the inner facing. With a lofty wool tie, this technique may not work; but, as we've always advised, when in doubt . . . *ask.*

The second element of construction to look for is the lining, known in the neckwear industry as the pocket tipping. It, too, aids in shape retention. A tie need not be lined from tip to tip; with a good inner facing this isn't really necessary. However, a quality tie should have a lining that runs at least from the bottom of the tie (the

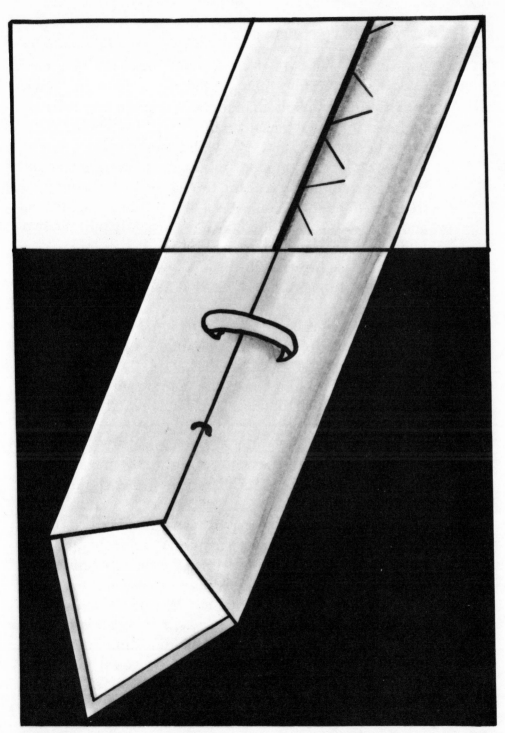

1. Slip-stitched.
2. Loop in which to insert small end of tie.
3. Bar-tacked.
4. Lined to the tip.

widest point) about six inches, and from the tie's narrowest point, or four inches. Most ties today aren't lined fully from top to bottom, and those that are are costly. A tie lined in silk, rather than a high-quality Bemberg or a rayon acetate, will also cost you more.

The third element to look for is slip stitching, a piece of thread inside the back of the tie that runs all the way up from top to bottom. You can see it if you turn the tie over and look at the back (you may have to gently pull the two folds of fabric away from each other); it will look like a piece of loose thread. But it actually serves an important purpose, acting as a backbone that helps the tie keep its shape.

Now check for bar tacking. A tie *must* be bar-tacked to have any level of construction quality. In bar tacking, a length of thread is sewn into the back of the tie, at the top and the bottom, to connect the outer seam to the inner part of the tie. The thread is approximately a quarter of an inch long, running horizontally across the tie at both ends. Some manufacturers put in bar tacking only at the wider end of the tie, but since the purpose of bar tacking is to help the tie keep its shape, we feel it should be at *both* ends.

A word on handmade versus machine-made ties. There are several terms you may encounter when shopping for a tie that may lead you to believe the tie was handmade. These include *hand tacking, hand-rolled,* and *hand-finished,* which refer to individual *steps* in making a tie. A tie may have been primarily machine-made, with only the finishing touches put in by hand. It's important to be aware of the difference, and to know you'll be paying extra for these hand touches that are largely of aesthetic appeal.

Earlier we said that the basic elements of construction that go into a tie have a great deal to do with the fabric used to make the tie. Here's a rundown on the most popular tie fabrics.

BASIC TIE FABRICS

Silk has historically been the number-one fabric used for men's ties. The "queen of fibers" is the strongest of all natural fibers, and ideal for this purpose because of its light weight, its durability, and its wrinkle resistance. Throughout history silk has been used for adding a luxury touch, the finishing touch, in a man's wardrobe. It has long been the most popular necktie fabric in the United States, not only for its luxury, but also for the practical fact of its excellent shape retention.

Silk

Foulard silk is one of the most commonly used tie fabrics in the United States. It has a rather flat or matte finish shine to it, is quite lightweight, and needs somewhat more tie construction than heavier weight silk.

Rep silk and *silk faille* are two somewhat heavier silk fabrics that have also traditionally been used in making ties. Rep silk fabric has narrow ribs that are spaced very close together, and silk faille has a very fine ridge to it, much like a very fine-line gabardine. For quite some time the traditional rep tie had very little construction put into it, because of its heavy nature. We feel, however, that both fabrics should have full construction to qualify as well-made ties. Heavy silk faille may not, in fact, require quite the heavy level of inner facing that other fabrics might, but it *should* be there, as should a lining (pocket tipping). Bar tacking and slip stitching *must* be there.

Shantung silk, often used for summer ties, originated in the Shantung Province of China. It has a rough, raised-weave effect that appears to have imperfections in it—knots, clumps, and bumps. These aren't, in fact, imperfections at all, but deliberate textural interest added through the weaving technique. It will appear, when you look at it closely, that some of the threads are thicker than others. This, again, is the *nature* of the silk.

Because Shantung silk is used a great deal in summer ties, we think it too should have full construction, as it must contend with the same climatic stress that a summer suit does. Hot, muggy summer days cause accelerated wrinkling and mussing. Good solid construction will help the tie retain its shape.

Crepe (or crepe de Chine) is a silk that has long been popular in Europe, but has only recently seen a rise in popularity here in the States. The main reason it hasn't been grandly popular here is, we think, that crepe ties are necessarily expensive. Crepe has a grainy, crinkly surface and is very lightweight, and so each silk crepe tie must be cut individually—unlike, say, foulards, a dozen of which can be cut on a machine at one time. Thus the labor and construction costs of crepe ties are automatically higher, and these costs go directly into the final price tag.

Crepe is a very dry and at the same time slippery fabric that absolutely must have a lining in order to retain its shape. Because of crepe's nature, and the amount of proper construction it requires, crepe ties tend to be the most expensive of all.

Silk, in fact, is indeed the most expensive of all the fibers used in making neckties. This is based in great part on the fact that the demand for silk as a luxury fiber has increased throughout the years, and the supply of silk has not met the demand. Thus, in much the same way wool is a luxury item in a suit for many men, silk is the predominant luxury fabric for neckwear.

Wool requires its own level of construction and brings with it its own set of problems in a tie. There are two different types of wool ties—wool knit and wool woven—and each has its own story.

Wool

With a *knit* wool tie, frequently worn with a tweed jacket, one of the biggest problems is that it can stretch out of shape very quickly. This is simply because it has been *knitted*. Knitted garments are not as stable or stress-resistant as woven garments; because of their looped nature of construction, they tend to stretch out rather easily.

So when you're buying a wool knit tie, one of the key elements of construction to look for is a tightly constructed neck band. In fact, the neck band itself should have a piece of woven fabric running along the inside of it, to absorb pressure when you tie the tie.

A wool *woven* tie is, as we've said, a different story. It is heavy by nature and requires less construction. For instance, a wool woven tie with a good inner facing needn't really be lined all the way through. In wool, one of the problems that occurs with too much construction is that the tie becomes bulky, uncomfortable, and unworkable around your neck.

All-cotton is another popular tie fabric that can be difficult to work with. An all-cotton tie, like most cotton

Cotton

garments, is mainly for summer wear, and the summer climate takes its toll on cotton neckwear as much as it does on those other garments.

A cotton tie wrinkles badly, so the construction that goes into it is extremely important. The fabric must be heavy enough, on its own, to maintain an independent level of shape retention. Obviously, we are not referring to shirting-weight cotton here, but a heavier variety. The tie must also be correctly constructed on the inside.

A problem common to cotton ties is an inner facing that has been put in poorly—that has not been fastened securely or in conformity with the shell fabric. What often happens in this case is that the inner facing becomes twisted, so that the inner facing pulls in one direction and the tie itself in another.

Polyester   Polyester, of course, has had its role to play in neckwear, too. After many, many years of men's ties being constructed with nothing but pure finish fibers, the introduction of polyester brought a whole new dimension of wearability to the neckwear industry.

The greatest advantage of polyester in menswear in general has always been its excellent shape-retention qualities. So, introduced into neckwear, polyester made a great deal of sense. Damage from the stress involved in the wearing of a tie—the knotting and constant pulling— could be allayed considerably by the use of polyester. And although polyester can present comfort problems when used in other garments (hot in summer, cold in winter), such problems can't occur with a purely decorative item such as a necktie.

Also, because it tends to be heavier by nature, polyester needs considerably less construction attention. This cuts the cost factor considerably. It is also less expensive than pure-finish fabrics. All this adds up to a less expensive, but totally serviceable, necktie.

One of the big problems with polyester, however, is that it doesn't take color, or dyes, as well as silk and other natural fibers do. Now, in a suit or a blazer, navy is navy, brown is brown, green is green, and black is black. Neckties don't work that way. Men simply do not limit themselves to basic, solid-colored neckties. They buy neckties with *colors* in them, and you just cannot get a lot of *true* colors in polyester. That's why a great number of ties are done today in poly/silk blends (as well as in polyester blended with other natural fibers).

The cost of a necktie is determined by a number of factors. We've talked about two of them—construction and fabric—but of the latter, in terms of pricing a tie, there is much more to say.

COST DETERMINANTS

The best tie fabrics originate in Italy—specifically in the city of Como, northeast of Milan. Here Italy's silk-screening industry is focused. When you buy a tie that was "screened" in Como, you are paying, first, for fabric exclusivity, an exclusivity well deserved by some of the finest printers and screeners in the world. A costly luxury, but it may be worth it to you if you love beautiful ties. Handscreening is the best, and you'll pay even more for it. The tie's label will often indicate whether the fabric was screened by hand or by machine.

Piecegoods, and how exclusive they are, affect the cost

of a tie. If a designer is doing a line of ties for which the piecegoods have been exclusively designed, you'll pay more. That means the line is being done in very small quantities. *You're* paying for the fact that the mill is only going to run a hundred rather than a thousand yards.

Designer name labels also add to the final cost of a necktie for the consumer. In fact, designer names seem to be more prevalent in neckwear than in any other area of menswear. Every time a designer's name appears on a garment, that designer must be paid a royalty on it. *You* help pay that royalty—in the price tag.

Here's a bit of inside information. For the most part, many designers don't actually design those ties they put their names on. They simply lend their names to a licensee. A consumer is often led to believe that because a designer has put his name on a tie, it is automatically a better tie. But this is not always the case. Here, again, is perceived value versus actual value. Don't be suckered in. If it's a quality tie, in the final analysis it really doesn't matter whether that designer's name appears on it or not.

MAINTENANCE Once you've bought what you know to be a quality tie, *always* have it dry-cleaned. Forget what the tag may say about washability. Any garment that can be washed can be dry-cleaned. Spend the extra money—it's worth it.

5. Outerwear

FUNCTIONALISM and utility are the key words to keep in mind when shopping for quality outerwear. The purpose of outerwear is to protect other items of your wardrobe—and you—from the elements. One of the problems men are faced with is garments that carry the claim of being able to do *everything*: the all-weather coat, the all-season suit. To the manufacturer this means less inventory to worry about. To the stores it means having to carry less stock. So if a salesperson can push the idea of buying an all-purpose garment on you, he will.

From our experience, however, it's a concept that rarely works. We aren't pushing the idea of a vast wardrobe of outerwear pieces; it's just that, for day-to-day wear, one garment simply can't meet all your needs. First, if you wear the same item every day, you won't get as much wear out of it as you should. Outerwear contends with far more day-to-day stress than other items in your wardrobe. Second is the question of appropriateness. You probably won't want to wear a raincoat or a nylon windbreaker over your suit when you spend an evening out on the town; nor would you very likely wear a tennis ensemble to the opera. Some garments just can't be pressed into service to meet every need, seasonally or acceptably.

Something else to keep in mind when buying outerwear in general is the recent trend toward making outerwear more sportswear-oriented, which means much more designer influence and detailing. Just be aware that you'll be paying for fashion as much as for function and utility. A basic outerwear piece, if well made, can meet your practical requirements; a fashion piece may not, and yet you'll be paying for those extra zippers, extra pockets, piping, and so on. They're nice touches, but you must ask yourself if they really have much to do with making the garment better. An interestingly detailed raincoat that isn't impervious to water, or an overcoat in a beautiful fabric that doesn't keep you warm, is no value.

To get the most value and quality for the money you're spending, *plan*. Buy outerwear according to the individual purpose each item will serve and the demands your lifestyle will place on it.

Before we talk about quality construction in outerwear, here's a rundown of the basic categories.

TOP COATS AND OVERCOATS Increasingly, the terms "topcoat" and "overcoat" are being used interchangeably today, but the two garments aren't really interchangeable in terms of the purpose each was designed to serve in your wardrobe.

Both garments are meant to be worn over a suit. A topcoat, however, is lighter in weight than an overcoat because it is designed to be worn over your suit in the early spring, when the air still has a chill to it. An overcoat is a winter coat, designed to be worn over your suit in the coldest weather.

What the two garments have in common is that they are both tailored in construction. Originally, the work that went on in a topcoat shop (where both topcoats and overcoats were made) was very similar to the work that went on in a suit shop: tailoring attention to the collar, the lapel, the sleeves, the shoulder. The cut-make-and-trim costs of these coats were quite substantial.

Today, topcoats and overcoats are really a dying breed, and there are very few *real* topcoat factories operating in the United States. The demise of the topcoat is due in great part to the influx of raincoat-type garments into the market (which we'll discuss later), and the prohibitive cut-make-and-trim costs.

As the costs of fully constructed topcoats spiraled, and as consumer tastes changed, outerwear manufacturers began to offer coats that had less construction, but had been made with better fabrics. This meant not having to deal with the numerous standard elements of construction that go into a fully tailored garment: inner canvas, certain shoulder treatments, perhaps twenty-two pressing steps. This resulted in fewer cut-make-and-trim costs, and labor costs in general—savings that went into buying better fabrics.

RAINCOATS

Rainwear has made great inroads into both the topcoat and the outerwear markets today, because the raincoat has assumed the role of "a coat for all seasons." The zip-out lining can be removed for warmer weather and zipped back in for colder weather. Another reason the raincoat has been able to assume this role of wardrobe chameleon is styling. Raincoats have generally been made in rather dark, conservative colors, and been designed to resemble the topcoat or overcoat.

OUTERWEAR We use the term "outerwear" in this chapter in its broad sense, but in the clothing industry it has a narrower sense: anything *other* than a topcoat, an overcoat, or a raincoat. The term refers to anything that was made in an outerwear plant in *cloth*, such as wool, poplin, or corduroy. Specific items of outerwear can be anything from a down jacket to a poplin golf jacket, a wool blouson, a nylon windbreaker, or a suburban coat.

Outerwear garments, in the narrow sense of the term, are not tailored garments. Outerwear construction is for less dressy, or more casual, garments.

FABRIC For many years, not just in outerwear but in most of the menswear market, all that was available to the consumer was all-natural fibers—all-wool, all-cotton, etc. These fabrics did a good job of protecting men from the elements, but the fabrics themselves took a beating. Outerwear in pure-finish fabric was always mussed and wrinkled, so cleaning and pressing the garment became a major consideration in buying outerwear.

Thus, the introduction of polyester, or polyester blended with natural fibers, was a boon to the outerwear market. It brought garments a level of shape retention that just could not be had with pure-finish fabrics, it lowered the cost of the garment, and it helped cut maintenance costs for the consumer. As other synthetic breakthroughs began to spill into the outerwear picture—such as the water-repellency treatment in raincoats—the benefits of synthetics and synthetic/natural blends were even more obvious.

A blended outerwear garment is almost always a value buy because you get the look of pure finish without having to pay the price, and you don't have to spend as much on maintenance and upkeep. Of course, an all-natural, pure-finish garment is indeed worth more, intrinsically, simply because it's pure fiber. But in terms of the overall durability and wearability of the garment itself, you'll get a better value in a blend.

Lest we come off as Pollyannas about polyester, we hasten to caution you regarding garments of all-polyester or with too much of this synthetic in them. An all-polyester garment can be cold in the winter and hot in the summer, and does not breathe well. You will also have the problem of not being able to find certain colors. Therefore we remind you to stay as basic as possible in color when a synthetic is predominant in the blend.

Topcoats and Overcoats

Before the advent of synthetic-and-natural-fiber blends, the only coats available to the consumer for many years were of pure wool. This was the industry standard, and for some men (who can afford it) it still is.

An all-wool garment will, of course, be more expensive than a poly/wool garment. A factor in this pricing is the actual weight of the piecegoods themselves. In topcoats and overcoats, 14 to 18 ounces per yard is the general range, though it can run as high as 22 ounces, as for some of the very heavy Donegal tweeds.

Is the fabric all-wool or a blend? Domestic or imported? Is it 14-ounce, 18-ounce, or 22-ounce? All these factors affect the price.

Most men may find that the standard 14-to-18-ounce coat is more than satisfactory for the climate they live in. For extremely cold winters a 22-ounce coat may be a necessity. Keep this factor in mind when deciding how heavy a coat you need.

Think twice also before buying a coat of too lofty a fabric—lofty meaning with a great deal of surface interest. You may like the visual effect, but these fabrics tend to wear down and look worn the fastest.

Definitely stay away from any loosely woven fabrics. These, too, may be visually interesting, but the stress and strain of everyday wear will cause the garment to be pulled out of shape. The tighter a fabric is woven, the better it can deal with day-to-day stress and the more resilient it will be. With a dress coat in a loosely woven fabric, the first things to go are the shoulder and the upper back and when these areas go, the garment is finished. It'll just hang on you, shapeless.

Another problem associated with loosely woven fabrics is pilling. All that surface interest can result in the fabric rubbing against itself or something else, like a car seat, and the shorter fibers in the yarn get pulled out of the material and end up tangled together in little balls, or "pills," on the surface. Nothing looks worse than a garment that is pilling, a sure sign that the garment is on its way out.

Most raincoats today are blends of polyester and cotton. *Raincoats*
There are still some of all-cotton, which cost more and require more upkeep, but they do breathe a little better than
those in polyester or polyester blends. The wiser investment, though, would seem to be a blend of polyester and a
natural fiber. It will have better shape retention, will require fewer trips to the cleaners, and will not present the
problem of getting true colors, as most of these garments
are offered in fairly basic, conservative colors anyway.

Most raincoat linings today are of a synthetic pile fabric, with acrylic predominating. From time to time a wool
lining is offered—a definite luxury, but when it gets
dirty, it *must* be dry-cleaned. The synthetic pile lining
will keep you just as warm as wool, is washable, and is as
durable as wool.

A word on washable raincoats and liners. Many raincoats are, but we feel it's a bad idea. First, certain oils
from your neck that get into the collar cannot be removed
totally by a washing machine. More important, if you do
wash the raincoat, you can't iron it properly yourself. For
that liner to fit back in, and continue to work properly in
the raincoat, you really must have it professionally
pressed.

Finally, be aware of the difference between a raincoat
that has been *rain-treated* and one that is *waterproof*.
Waterproof means that the garment has been coated in
such a way that it becomes impervious to water. This, of
course, also means that the garment does not breathe.
Rubber is waterproof, a rain *slicker* is waterproof, and if
you wear them for a lengthy period of time you melt in
them because they don't breathe. A raincoat should not

be waterproof but water-*repellent*. Usually it is treated with a substance known as Zepel, a trademarked chemical compound that simply creates a chemical shield around the fibers. This treatment also makes the fabric stain-repellent.

LEATHER, SUEDE, FUR, AND FUR-LINED GARMENTS

These are at the luxury end of the outerwear industry, and any sort of value judgment in terms of quality would be difficult. It's mostly a matter of what you like. So, we'll simply tell you what to look for in this area of outerwear, and why you'll pay what you will.

Leather and suede, of course, are skins and not fabrics. So let's talk hides, because in leather and suede garments what you're ultimately paying for is the quality of the hides used, and the cost of labor that went into making them into a garment.

Leather prices vary from the most expensive unborn calf all the way down to steer hide. The difference is the age of the animal, which affects the skin's grain. Needless to say, a garment made from unborn calf is softer and more supple than one made from steer hide. Obviously, a steer is an older animal, so the grain in the skin is larger, and there will be more scratches and scars.

Some skins are more precious than others, and will obviously cost you more. Also more expensive are fashion leathers—leathers that have been dyed, or embellished with nonfunctional trim. The *most* expensive leathers today come from Italy, where there are better skins and better factories. Many dyes used on suede and leather come from Europe only. A good amount of leather work is being done in the Far East today, because production is less expensive there. The work done there, on a whole, is quite adequate; just remember that you should be paying less for it.

Furs and pelts are at the extreme end of the luxury area of the outerwear market, and by nature of their price they are still the smallest part of that market. But interest in furs and fur-lined outer garments seems to be on the rise in menswear, so a bit of basic information on them seems to be in order. **FURS AND PELTS**

Fur garment manufacturing, and selling, is an art, much like diamond cutting and selling. In fact, one might compare buying a fur coat to buying a diamond—you're also buying the reputation of the furrier, just as you are that of the jeweler. With furs, most consumers are simply not in a position—not skilled or educated enough—to know exactly what it is they are buying; they would need years of experience to acquire that knowledge.

One would assume, however, that if you bought a diamond from, say, Tiffany's, you would get a better diamond than if you bought it "downtown" at a less reputable source. We feel that the same holds true for furs, so our advice is to shop around, first, for the *furrier*. Check out the reputation, then the furs.

Here are some tips and hints about the furs used most often in men's outerwear today. To begin with, some are simply more utilitarian than others.

Mink, for instance, wears like iron. There are various grades of mink, all at different price points.

Lynx, on the other hand, sheds very quickly. The fur is

long, silky, and usually a light grayish brown in color, with darker spots and stripes.

Beaver can also be a perishable pelt and is generally offered at comparably higher prices. The fur is usually thick and deep brown in color, but the most sought-after fur is brown with a blue cast to it.

Nutria comes in at rather comfortable price points and can wear nicely; the blue-brown color is preferred. Similarly, *muskrat* wears fairly well for the moderate prices it is offered at; stay away from garments made from the belly fur, however, because they don't fare as well as those made from the back of the animal. There will probably be a price variance from this standpoint as well.

Raccoon and *opossum* have reputations for holding up to wear well. Opossum can be moderately priced. *Rabbit* generally does not hold up terribly well, but there is a *sheared* rabbit, from France, that is gaining a good reputation for wear.

An increasing number of *fur-lined* garments are making an entry into the menswear market. They tend to be less expensive than full fur, they're lightweight (the shell is usually poplin or wool), they do keep you warm, and if the particular fur is strong, they'll wear well for a long time.

Fur, then, is the ultimate dressy outerwear garment. Furs are lightweight, they're luxurious, and they represent the ultimate in real clothing investment. If you buy a fur coat, know that you are going to wear it for a long, long time. Our advice, again, is to shop around, find a reputable furrier, and *then* select the garment.

As for the elements of construction to look for in these materials—leather, suede, or fur—we suggest that you look for the same elements we outline in the next section for outerwear in general. A raglan sleeve is as important, for example, in leather and suede as it is in cloth; a quality zipper is essential. With furs, make certain those pelts are sewn together well, and that there is no evidence whatsoever of loose threads.

Because of the role outerwear plays in your life—to protect you and your other garments from the various elements of nature—proper construction is essential. Topcoats and overcoats, for example, are fully constructed tailored garments, and a similar amount of construction should have gone into them as goes into a tailored suit.

STANDARD ELEMENTS OF QUALITY IN OUTERWEAR CONSTRUCTION

First, check the stitching. It should be tight and perfect. The more stitches per inch, the better. This is an area where we feel machine stitching is better than hand stitching; machines don't skip, and a more consistent stitching thoughout the garment will ultimately give it more strength.

Essentially, there are two basic collar treatments in outerwear: the lay-down collar, which looks much like the collar of a suit, and the *Balmaccan collar,* which is rounded. Whichever style you choose, keep in mind that the collar and the lapel are two key construction elements that must work right in order for the garment to do its work.

When you put the garment on, the collar and the lapel must lie perfectly flat and hug your neck closely. One reason for this is purely aesthetic; the other is practical: You don't want cold air going down your neck.

The felling material used in the collar (and this is especially true in topcoats) should be heavy enough to hold it down nice and flat. You should not expect a Balmaccan collar to lie as flat as a conventional collar, because of its stylistic nature, but there should definitely be enough inner lining on it to at least keep it down.

The shoulder area is another crucial construction element in the quality of an outerwear garment, as it plays a significant role in determining how the rest of the garment will function. The shoulder line should be straight and even; one shoulder should not droop lower than the other.

Two types of sleeve treatments come into play here: the raglan sleeve and the more common set-in sleeve.

The raglan sleeve dates back to the Crimean War, when Lord Raglan designed a sleeve that would allow his soldiers' shoulders greater freedom of movement on the battlefield. A raglan sleeve starts at the neck of the garment and runs down to where the armhole ends. There are two types of raglan sleeves, a full raglan and a split raglan. A split raglan simply has a seam that splits it down the middle.

In terms of functionalism, a raglan sleeve is preferable to a set-in sleeve, which does not afford the wearer the freedom of movement a raglan does. Raglan-sleeved outerwear garments seem to wear better.

Another element to check carefully in outerwear is the lining, and how it was put in. The lining in a fully constructed, tailored topcoat or overcoat should, of course, have been put in with the same level of quality and attention with which the lining of a suit is put in. It should be stitched in very carefully and evenly.

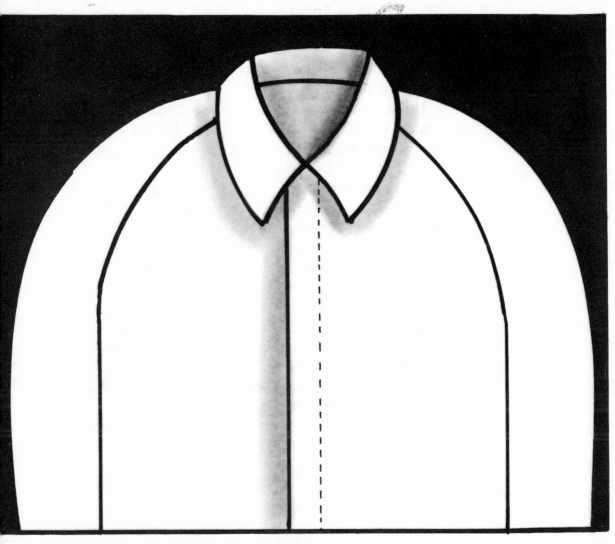

1. Collar lies flat, with sides evenly proportioned.
2. Raglan sleeve—deep enough to accommodate easy movement.
3. Fly front lies flat when coat is buttoned.

Jacket linings are usually sewn into the shell. In a poplin jacket or suburban coat, the pile lining has a facing sewn onto it.

Unlike the linings in raincoats, which usually zip or button in and out, outerwear jacket linings as a rule are put in permanently, so you should double-check the stitching to make certain the lining was put in securely. Also, make sure the lining has been cut, and put in, to correspond to the shell of the garment. There should be neither too much nor too little lining.

If you're looking at a raincoat, make note of how the lining hangs. It should be perfectly even, not longer in the back than in the front, or longer on one side than on the other.

Raincoat linings either zip in or button in. For zip-in linings, make sure the zipper is anchored securely onto the shell of the garment. Try the zipper itself. A cheap one is a fairly dependable sign that the garment is cheap all over. Remember that a raincoat with a zip-in lining is meant to be worn all year round; the zipper must therefore be of the highest quality, and work well. Also, don't buy the coat if the zipper is totally exposed. There should be a little covering, like a pant fly, between that zipper and you, simply to protect you from the metal.

If the raincoat has a button-in liner, make sure the buttons and their holes are spaced perfectly evenly; this will help you avoid pulling the fabric too tight, or getting an overlap of it.

Back to zippers in general for a moment. For any outerwear garment that zips, the zipper must be heavy and durable. If you're looking at a big bulky jacket, for instance, and it has a tiny little zipper in it, forget it. Look

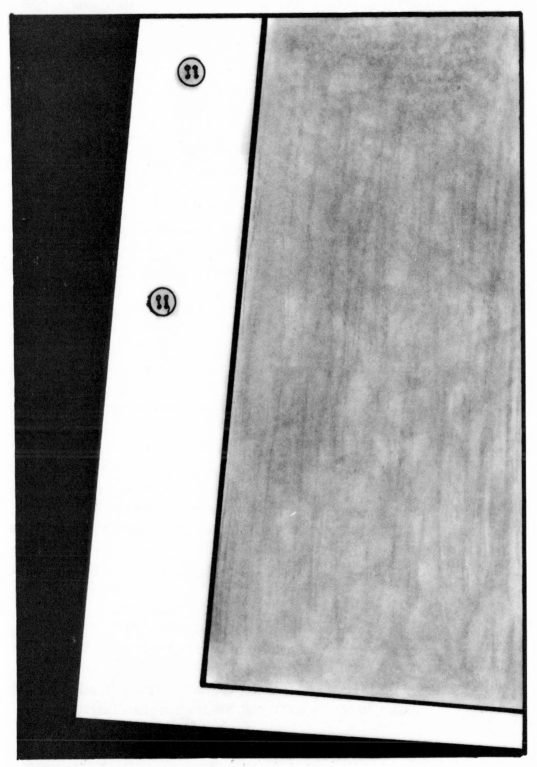

1. Inside buttons firmly anchored.
2. Lining set in smoothly and evenly (whether button, zip, or permanent).
3. Lining fits fabric shell appropriately.

for a strong zipper, an appropriate zipper for the garment it has to serve. Conversely, a lightweight nylon windbreaker shouldn't have the same zipper a hefty wool jacket might have.

Some outerwear garments have two-way zippers. This means you can unzip them from the bottom as well as from the top.

Buttons, in general, must also be durable. On outerwear, it is especially important that buttonholes be well finished. A big button going through a shoddily finished hole (too small, or with loose threads) will cause the hole to unravel.

The anchoring of the button must be extremely strong. Check the button neck, where it attaches to the garment. If the neck appears too long, too short, or simply weak, don't buy the garment.

A nice touch in an outerwear garment, and indicative of quality, is a fly front, a piece of fabric that goes over the closure itself, whether a zipper or buttons, simply to give the garment a more finished look. If the garment has one, make sure it's neatly and well stitched, with a good number of stitches. A fly front must lie perfectly flat.

Pockets are crucial on outerwear. They hold hands, gloves, cigarettes, keys, spare change, and many other items, all of which cause stress. Make sure the pocket linings have been stitched tightly and evenly, with no loose threads.

ELEMENTS OF FIT Outerwear generally comes sized the same way a suit does: essentially, sizes 36 to 46. However, some outerwear pieces today are offered in small, medium, and large sizes—a money-saver for the manufacturer. You

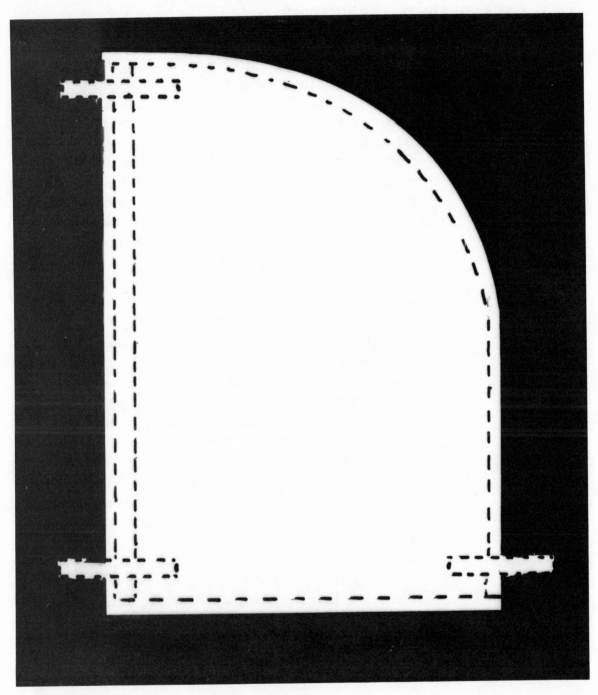

1. Outerwear pockets firmly attached to coat.
2. Reinforced at key stress points with additional fabric.
3. Pocket lining should be of tightly woven fabric.
4. Pocket size should easily accommodate hand.

may happen to fit well into one of these sizes; just be aware that you should not necessarily be paying the same price for a garment sized in this way as for one marked with a specific size.

In terms of the fit itself, the shoulders are crucial. When you put on a piece of outerwear, make certain you have enough room to move freely and comfortably in it. By this, we don't mean that there should be excess bulk in the back or the front, but that the shoulders do not restrict free and easy movement. The shoulder should rest evenly and smoothly, and the garment should not pull out of shape when you rotate or pull with your arms.

Make sure you'll be able to put the garment on over whatever it is you'll ordinarily be wearing under it. Move around in the garment—move your arms forward and back; bend from the middle. Then sit down. Move your arms again.

The sleeves should, of course, be long enough, and neither too tight nor too full. They should comfortably accommodate the movement of your arms.

Often a blouson jacket will have knitted ribbing at the end of the sleeve and at the bottom of the jacket. This ribbing must be tight—at the cuffs, to keep the cold air from going up your arm; and at the bottom of the jacket, to insure that it will always fit snugly, as its design intends.

The length of a garment is naturally a factor in fit, and affects whether the garment will work right. A topcoat or overcoat, since it is worn over a suit for warmth, should, of course, adequately encompass the suit jacket; it mustn't be too short. A raincoat should give you protec-

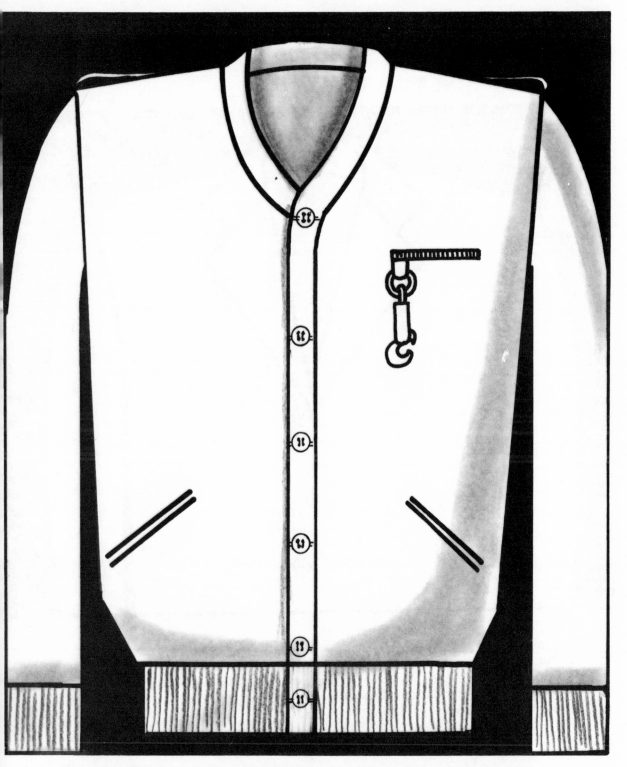

1. Knit cuffs and bottom tight and snug-fitting even after repeated cleanings.
2. Sporty decorative touch adds higher duty if garment is imported.
3. Buttons firmly anchored, with cleanly finished buttonholes.

1. Collar hugs the neck and lies flat.
2. Lapel lies flat.
3. Buttons securely anchored and buttonholes firmly sewn.
4. Front of coat (closure) lies flat over your suit coat with no pulling.
5. Shoulder seam lies flat and smooth.
6. Sleeve set in with no puckering.

tion from the rain, and so if it rises much above your knee, it doesn't make much sense; at the knee or just below is wisest.

A blouson-length jacket must fit over your waist. If it doesn't, every time you move forward it's going to pull up over the top of your pants. It won't be long enough to keep you warm as it was designed to do in the winter, and the ribbing or banding at the bottom that was intended to keep out the cold will be useless. When you try on a blouson jacket in the store, stand in it and make sure it fits snugly around the hips.

6. Knitwear

THE WORD "knitting" derives from an old Anglo-Saxon word, *cnyttan*, which means to weave threads by hand. We use the term today to describe a method of fabric construction in which, instead of actually weaving fibers into fabric, one or more yarns are interlocked in a series of loops. The original process was accomplished by hand, with the knitter working on a pair of needles that were either round or straight, slipping stitches between the two needles, adding a new stitch with each exchange. Today, of course, we have knitting machines that are quite proficient at doing what once only hands could do. Indeed, while an element of hand knitting still exists, most knitwear today is created on machines.

Because of their "looped" nature, knitted garments drape well, breathe well, and are less susceptible to wrinkling. They also have great insulating qualities and bring with them a general, all-around sense of comfort. In essence, knits have their own separate and distinct personalities, serve their own wardrobe purposes, and therefore really shouldn't be compared with other fabrics.

Almost any item of wearing apparel you can find in your wardrobe can be, and has been, produced in a knitted fabric. Knitwear, in its broadest generic sense, covers everything from a pair of socks to suits, pants, shirts, and sweaters. For our purposes here, however, and for the sake of clarity, we'll use the term "knitwear" to refer to men's shirts (including T-shirts but not undershirts) and sweaters.

The knitwear industry in this country has its very own nature, and in order to maneuver effectively and most cost-efficiently within it, you need to know how it thinks and works. So let's talk first about pricing considerations in general.

WHAT YOU'LL PAY, AND WHY

From the outset, what it costs a manufacturer to produce a knitted garment is a key factor in what you, the consumer, will have to pay for it. In knitwear—especially in the U.S. market—there are several important variables that affect a manufacturer's cut-make-and-trim costs.

Actually, the U.S. knitwear industry, as a working industry *within* this country, has declined considerably. Three factors play significant roles in the diminished capacity of the knitwear industry here. First, labor costs; second, we simply do not have the quality and diversity of yarn that are available elsewhere in the world; and third, we have failed to develop the type of knitwear machinery required to execute the fine-quality and highly sophisticated stitches so many consumers want.

The highest-quality yarns, as well as the most advanced and intricate stitching techniques, are found in Europe—and the Europeans exact a high price for them. Simply stated, knitwear from Europe continues to be the best on the market, but prices on it are higher than ever, and continue to rise at a steady rate.

A few words on knitwear from the Far East. Manufacturers began moving to the Orient for knitwear in the late fifties, and continued to do so through the sixties and seventies. Hong Kong was the original knitwear mecca, but today the entire Far East caters to manufacturers' knitwear needs—Taipei, South Korea, Sri Lanka, Singapore, and the Philippines, to name a few. This exodus to the Orient was based on two major factors: Labor was cheap, and the cost of yarn (bought in bulk) was lower than in Europe.

In the beginning, Hong Kong, with its inexpensive labor, was able to offer the consumer a very basic sweater at the lowest of prices; unfortunately, overall quality was poor. Since then, Hong Kong has developed the sophistication of its machinery and the quality of its product to the point that many designer-label knitwear items are being produced there.

Most of the knitwear you have to choose from today is imported. This includes the products of domestic companies, who must pass the cost of importing along to the consumer in a garment's final markup.

Another word about imported knitwear, and how the price tag is affected. Since European knitwear is so costly to begin with, stores can't really do an effective sales promotion on it—but knitwear from the Far East fits this purpose perfectly. What you should be aware of, where knitwear quality and price tags are concerned, is how certain stores handle sales promotions.

How do you know when a sale is really a sale?

Here's how it often works. Let's say a store buys a Shetland sweater from a brand-name U.S. manufacturer for $10 and then retails the sweater at $20. At the same time, a large department store goes into the Far East and gets basically the same Shetland sweater, but, because the store bought in vast quantities, is able to bring it in at, say, $6.50. The store then says that the sweater retails or sells for $20. The *comparable* value of the sweater may be $20, but in reality it is selling for only $13, or twice what the store paid, the usual markup. The store may even advertise the sweater as "regularly $20, on sale for $12.99"—the legitimate selling price! And so this sale simply isn't a sale at all.

It's a sales tactic used in menswear, womenswear, and various other areas of retail. Of course, a retailer has a right to sell his merchandise at whatever price he sees fit—and he really has no obligation to tell you what he bought it for. But you, as a consumer, have a right to know what you're paying for. Stores frequently affix a specific label to merchandise they bought in the Far East. Ask salespeople what this label is (a new brand, or a store label). Keep in mind that the store may be doing a heavy promotional pitch on it.

Yarns Along with general production costs, a number of other factors affect a knitted garment's final quality and price tag. Let's start with yarns.

For many years in the knitwear business, one of the key factors that determines price has been the type of yarn that is used. Just as wool in a suit is more expensive than texturized polyester, wool in knitwear is generally more expensive than cotton. Wool has always been the key yarn used for sweaters, because it has a natural warmth and breathability (when you perspire, you're perspiring *through* the wool).

Various qualities of wool are available to manufacturers for producing sweaters. In the United States the yarns most commonly sold are lambswool and Shetland. Lambswool, as its name implies, is taken from a lamb rather than a sheep, and is softer. Generally, Shetland wool is used in moderate-priced sweaters.

As we mentioned earlier, the best wools in general come from Europe; the best lambswool and Shetland come from England, Scotland, and Italy. Merino wool, often referred to as "Botany wool" because of the area in Australia where it comes from, is also a good, durable, wonderfully elastic wool. It is taken from the merino sheep of that region.

Cotton is the second most frequently used fiber, especially for summerweight knitted garments. Like wool, it's absorbent and comfortable to wear.

Various stitching techniques are employed to create a knitted cotton garment. In the pique stitch, the yarn is combed, then woven in such a way as to create various textures. In the interlock stitch, the yarns are interlocked on a machine that has alternating units of both short and long needles; the result is a garment that has a firm texture and good elasticity.

Cotton lisle is more than just a stitch, because of the

way it's woven. A two-ply cotton yarn is combed, then twisted wet. The result is a firm, compact yarn that is soft and silky to the touch. Cotton lisle has a very fine quality, and is always used in the most expensive garments.

For mercerized cotton, the yarn itself has been mercerized, or treated in a manner that lends it both sheen and softness. Mercerized cotton is also used in somewhat more expensive garments.

Pure-finish yarns were always used in the highest quality and most expensive knitted garments. As the cost of these yarns rose, the introduction of synthetics became a very important part of the manufacturer's mix.

When we refer to synthetics in knitwear, essentially we're talking about acrylic, polyester, and nylon. The introduction of synthetics has less to do with increasing shape retention where sweaters are concerned than cutting the cost of using expensive, pure-finish yarns. It's true that an acrylic knit can be washed more easily—a maintenance factor you'll want to consider—but for the most part, acrylic and polyester are mixed with wool and summerweight fabrics, such as cotton, simply to bring the cost down.

Occasionally you'll find nylon in a sweater. This can be an advantage if the garment is made primarily of a natural fiber and is very loosely knitted; the nylon will enhance the garment's shape retention, so that the standard points of stress on loose knits, elbows and shoulders, will hold up better.

Remember that with synthetics in knitwear (as with synthetics in other garments) you'll have a problem with yarns dying up in certain colors. You'll never get as true a color with a synthetic as you will in natural fibers. This doesn't mean the color will necessarily be undesirable, just that you run the risk of getting brassiness in certain colors; burgundies often come up cranberry, yellow can go lemony. It's also difficult to get a really good navy, since this color, too, will come up brassy.

The level of design sophistication that goes into a knitted garment will play a significant role in determining its price. A basic lambswool sweater, with no special colors or pattern, will naturally cost less than one into which intricate work has gone. If you love aesthetically beautiful, interestingly twisted and colored yarns, you'll have to pay for them. *Modeling*

An unusual or complex pattern automatically elevates the price of a sweater. Let's say you come across a sweater with four separate patterns made out of the same yarn, with an additional diagonal or crisscross design in it. You're not only going to have to pay for the concept—the actual creativity of the designer—but you're also going to have to pay for the element of work that went into executing the designer's concept.

The more detailed the modeling in a knitted garment, the more costly it will be, both to make and to buy. Elaborate necklines, leather or suede trim, an inset, placed motifs—all represent an expensive proposition to the manufacturer, partly because, for each added detail, the machine frequently must be stopped and then restarted again.

Further, any kind of hand detailing will drive the cost of the garment up. A hand intarsia sweater, for instance, will run you more than a simple, basic model, based strictly on the manner in which the pattern was created. Intarsia (derived from the Italian word for "inlay") is a flat-knit fabric, where solid-colored patterns (usually geometric in nature) have been knitted in. A placed motif on a sweater will also cost more if it was hand-done. A placed motif is a particular design or symbol that is placed in one specific area of the sweater's body—say an eagle in the center of the back, or a nautical design in the shoulder area. Whether the motif was put in by hand or by machine, the final cost of the garment will rise correspondingly.

A few words on the subject of handwork in knitwear. Three terms you may encounter are "handknits," "handloomed," and "handframed." A handknit is a fabric that was knitted entirely by hand, as opposed to having been done on a machine. References to handlooming or handframing, however, do not imply an entirely hand-done process, and don't be misled into thinking so.

Here's how it breaks down. A hand*loomed* sweater is made on a knitting machine, but there is a person standing at the machine throughout the process, and he or she throws the bobbin. This additional human touch adds a bit more cost to the garment's final markup, but it adds an element of quality control, too.

Hand*framing* refers to a *construction* process. Imagine a pattern, or frame, on which various parts of a sweater pattern are placed—let's say it's an intarsia pattern, with lots of little diamonds. Once all the diamonds have been placed on the frame, they are put together by hand. Thus, a handframed sweater. But don't be led to believe the sweater was *completely* handmade.

Construction Methods Essentially, there are two ways in which knit garments are made: cut-and-sewn and full-fashioned. Full-fashioned means that the entire garment has been fashioned out of one yarn, knitted in a continual process, from the first stitch to the last. A cut-and-sewn garment is basically what its name implies; the fabric was knitted on a machine, cut into pieces, and the pieces were sewn together to achieve the garment's ultimate shape.

Full-fashioned knitted garments have always been considered to be the best, because you get a nicer-shaped, better-constructed item. The quality is in the time and concern that went into making it.

A cut-and-sewn knit is not, however, necessarily cheap. For instance, a shirt or sweater design that combines both knit and woven elements *must* be cut and sewn; there's no way around it.

Here's an example of what we're talking about. Let's take a sweater with a yellow body and a black collar. If a manufacturer were really aiming for top quality, he would simply stop the machines at the collar, put in black yarn, and restart the machines. But few manufacturers would go about it that way. Rather, they would stop the machines before producing the collar, knit the black collar separately, and sew it on. Even though some waste occurs, this cut-and-sew method is still a less expensive means of producing the garment; a shortcut, as it were.

HOW TO BUY A QUALITY SWEATER

Before you even try on a sweater, examine its neckline. Regardless of its style—crewneck, V-neck, or boatneck—the neckline must be even, without even the hint or suggestion of loose yarn. On a knitted garment, loose yarn can mean only one thing: It's unraveling! Once it's started, it'll keep happening, so steer clear of it.

The neckline on a sweater should be firm. A sweater's neckline gives the garment its definition, personality, and style. With turtlenecks, make doubly certain the neckline has a natural spring to it, that it returns, naturally, to its original shape. Otherwise, that neckline is going to start drooping very soon, resulting in sloppiness.

Check the garment's hem and cuffs. They will either be knitted or finished. If the cuff or hems are knitted, or ribbed, it means the knitting process was just continued down, and a different stitch was used to finish it off. With a finished cuff or hem the knitting process was simply stopped at the bottom, then the fabric is turned under and sewn up.

Now consider comfort. Crucial to the fit of a sweater is the amount of room you have to move in it. Sweaters, as opposed to some T-shirts, should never be tight or constricting. If it's too tight on you, you'll run into the problem of the garment's losing its shape. Remember that the shoulder and elbow areas are the two major points of stress on a sweater. You move from the shoulders and the elbows, and knits especially, which do not have the resistance woven fabrics do, need room in these areas.

Another important aspect of fit in a sweater is the amount of room from the shoulder to the arm. If a sweater is too tight under the arm, by the very nature of the way our arms work and move, there will be constant heavy stress for that area. For the same reason, make certain there is enough room at the shoulder, in the back of the sweater.

On the other hand, a sweater should not have arms that are cut too full, or that drop too far down, giving a sloppy appearance.

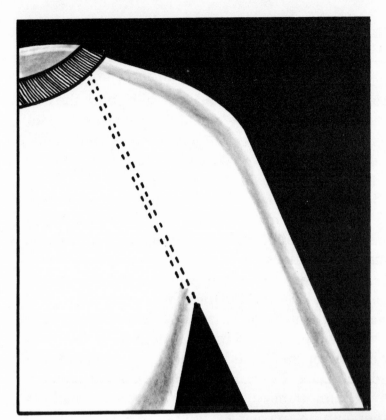

1. Full-fashioned sleeve.
2. Tight ribbing at neck.

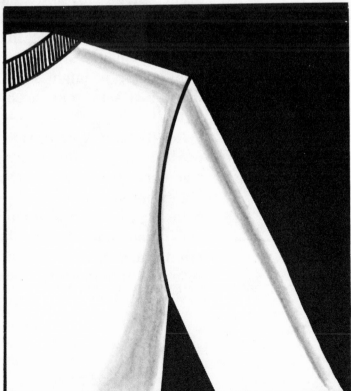

1. Set-in sleeve—smooth
   with no puckering.
2. Large enough to comfortably
   accommodate arm movement.

Remember that a raglan sleeve will always fit more comfortably than a set-in sleeve. Coinciding with the natural structure of your body and the movement of your muscles, a raglan sleeve permits easier, more comfortable movement. Raglan sleeves cost more to make, and are always found on full-fashion garments.

The fit of a sweater is quite different from that of other knitted items. Sweaters are sportswear, and sportswear items generally needn't fit on the same levels of exacting specification as tailored apparel and dress shirts. Traditionally, sportswear, including sweaters, has always run small, medium, large, and extra-large.

Keep in mind when you're trying a sweater on for size, however, that there are no rating standards in the knitwear industry for small, medium, and large; they are general and not exact. Every manufacturer does it his own way. A medium to one man is not necessarily a medium to another, and if you wear a small in some garments (say a shirt), you do not necessarily wear a small in a sweater. Remember that, except in the case of some summer-weight garments, sweaters are usually worn over a shirt. Your body type might be small, but the shirt adds a layer that the sweater must accommodate properly and comfortably.

Additionally, garments manufactured elsewhere in the world often fit differently than they would if they were made here, with the American man's body type in mind. For example, garments that are made in France and Italy naturally fit a bit differently because they were designed and manufactured with the French or Italian man in mind. American manufacturers tend to be a bit more consistent in fit than manufacturers overseas. This, of course, does not imply that something produced elsewhere in the world is necessarily inferior—just that it's produced differently, and you should take this into consideration when shopping.

Also, when trying knitwear on for proper fit, keep in mind that the designer of the garment may have wanted something that was big and bulky, but that in his mind the size was still a small. Bulk, remember, is shape, and can still be sized as small. This is a designer's way of making a fashion statement, and here, of course, is where stylistic considerations must come into wise decision-making on your part.

KNIT SHIRTS

A knit shirt can be made in the same way a sweater can: full-fashioned, or cut-and-sewn. If a shirt design includes a woven collar, placket, or other such detail, cut-and-sewn may be the only way.

The crucial stress points on a knitted shirt are the neckline, shoulderline, chest, and arm area. Try the shirt on and check these areas as you would a sweater.

Next, examine the collar closely. It should be evenly finished, meaning no loose yarn or threads. If it was cut-and-sewn, it should be attached cleanly and evenly, and it should have a firm, elastic quality. Pull the collar gently; when it is released, it should spring right back into its original shape and position.

The placket should lie smooth and flat, and any stitching should be cleanly finished. A good indication of quality is a lining material stitched into the placket.

All buttonholes should be cleanly finished, with no loose threads.

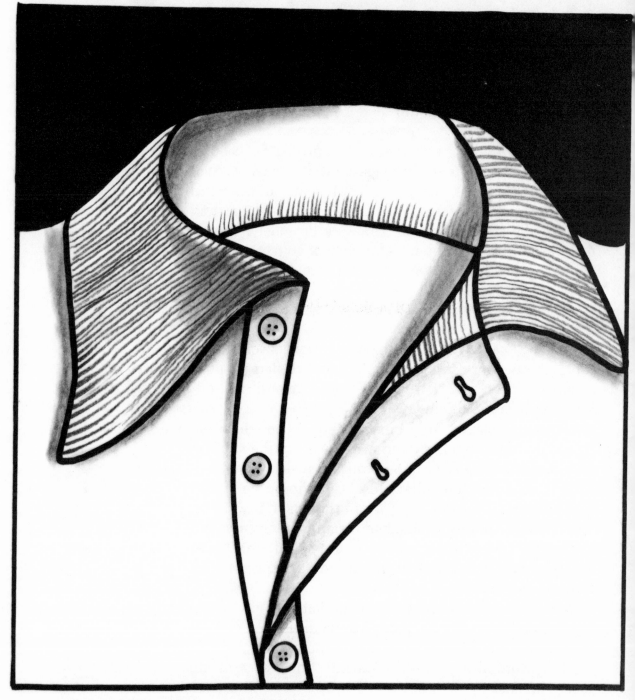

1. Tightly ribbed collar, evenly shaped.
2. Strongly sewn buttonholes, cleanly finished.
3. Firmly anchored buttons.
4. Buttonhole should match button, for a smooth front.
5. Sewn-down inside placket.
6. Lined placket.

The buttons should be securely attached, or anchored.

The sleeves should accommodate your arms comfortably, fitting neither too tightly nor too loosely. A plain hemmed sleeve must be cleanly finished; another good sign of quality is a healthy count of stitches. A ribbed sleeve must be tight and firm. Once again, in terms of fit, we still think a raglan sleeve is best.

Often, knit shirts with cut-and-sewn rib bottoms fail to lie as flat as full-fashioned garments. For this reason, make sure the ribbing is firm and tight. Stretch it, and see that it springs back into position. Elasticity is a natural property of knitted garments, and if something as elemental and crucial as this does not exist, you don't want the garment.

When you're trying the shirt on, make sure that the placket is lying flat and smooth, and that there is absolutely no evidence of puckering, wrinkling, or bubbling. The fit should be comfortable and nonrestricting, and when you move in the shirt, it should neither gape nor pull. The seams should be flat and even, and the body of the shirt should exhibit no evidence of wrinkling or pulling. Look also for a comfortable fit across the chest; it should be neither too full nor too tight. Keep in mind what we said earlier about sizing specifications in knitwear. Try it on, because what you wear in a woven shirt won't necessarily accommodate you properly in a knitted shirt. It should not be cut too high under the arm, nor should the sleeve area drop too low.

In a T-shirt or other form-fitting style, the neckline and sleeves (if finished with an elastic) are crucial areas, so construction quality is essential. The greater the number of stitches in these areas, the better the garment was made, and the better it will launder.

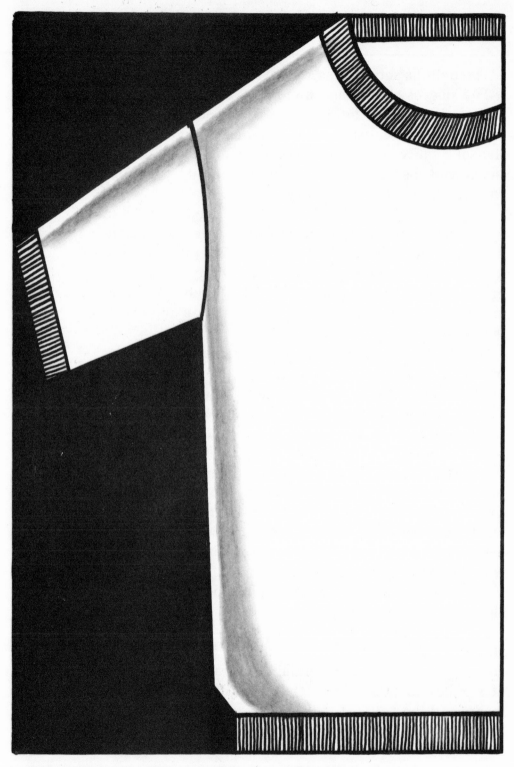

1. *Tightly knitted sleeve hem, neck band, and bottom—*
   should keep tight elastic quality after repeated launderings.
2. *Set-in sleeve—smooth with no puckering.*

Test the elasticity of the neckline in the same manner. Then, when you have it on, make certain that it fits comfortably across the chest and under the arms.

HOW TO CARE FOR KNITTED GARMENTS

Any garment that can be washed can be dry-cleaned. We're not suggesting that you run out and spend hundreds of dollars every month on dry-cleaning your entire wardrobe. But to give you the most value, pure-finish fabrics, especially in sweaters, really should be dry-cleaned.

One of the factors to take into consideration when shopping for knitwear is colorfastness. It is true that just about all T-shirts are machine-washable, and some cotton sweaters can also be washed. But the fact remains that you can't test a garment's colorfastness before you buy it and launder it. If it is dyed purple, there's just no way of knowing whether it will remain that shade of purple until it has been washed. A quality garment should be colorfast, and there should be a label inside that tells you so.

Today, of course, you can get sweaters, in all colors, that are both washable (in terms of shape retention and shrinkage) and colorfast. There are even some wool sweaters that can be washed. Most manufacturers specifically tell you if a sweater is washable or not—and they're specific because they don't want the garment brought back.

If you are going to wash, you're usually safer if you *handwash*. In which case, never wring the garment out, but squeeze it gently and lay it out flat and even on clean bath towels so that it can dry back naturally into its original shape. This process, of course, is done out of contact with direct sunlight and heat.

Finally, to increase the life of your knitted garments, never hang them. This can cause the hemline to droop and can pull the entire garment out of shape.

Knits should be folded and put away in their own drawer; or, if they absolutely must be stored in a closet, hang them, *folded,* over a padded rod or hanger.

7. Related Separates

RELATED separates, in the most elemental definition of the term, are sportswear component pieces that relate to each other via color. The idea originated in womenswear, through the concept of coordinates—two articles of wearing apparel, usually a top and a bottom, merchandised as one look, in one package, and ordinarily sold at one price. More often than not, the two coordinate pieces were dyed to match.

The introduction of related separates brought a new dimension of flexibility and interest to the coordinates concept. Unlike coordinates, related separates are rarely dyed to match, but have an aesthetically consistent color theme that causes each garment in the separates package to relate to the others. If the color palette for a separates package is gray, navy, and gold, that doesn't mean that every item in it must be gray, navy, and gold; these are the base colors, and each garment's color must be keyed to them. An aesthetically consistent color statement is the key.

Related separates also differ from coordinates in that while both are merchandised to coordinate, separates are sold separately rather than as a package. The beauty of this system is that a man can match a small top with a medium bottom—or whatever combination his body type requires—and still get the same look.

WHAT YOU'RE ACTUALLY PAYING FOR In menswear, the related separates department encompasses four basic clothing classifications: sweaters (knitwear); woven shirts and tops; slacks (bottomweights); and jackets (outerwear). From time to time, some manufacturers offer sportcoats that are specifically designed to relate to the other pieces, but this classification is minimal (and quite expensive). More on this a little later.

What are you actually paying for when you shop in the related separates department? You're paying for a concept, and what it cost to actualize it. You really aren't paying for the individual garments based on what they're actually worth; you could do that if you bought them in their parent departments. You're paying for the time and skill that went into putting the four classifications of clothing together for you in an aesthetically consistent color statement. Since a great portion of what is offered in related separates carries a designer name, you're also helping to pay the royalty fee that must be paid on any garment carrying that name. And, finally, you're paying for the convenience of not having to coordinate an outfit from the parent departments. You're saving time and effort—but are you saving money?

One of the major factors that determine what you'll pay for related separates begins at the manufacturing level. Most separates manufacturers today do not own their own factories. They contract their work out and must pay a fee to the contractor—a cost that is passed along to the retailer, who passes it on to us.

Another factor that has an impact on pricing is where the merchandise was produced. Most separates manufacturers today produce their lines in the Orient, for much the same reason knitwear manufacturers do: labor costs. The hitch is that, in the Orient, manufacturers are accustomed to doing larger runs of merchandise; but, by the very nature of the related separates concept, *smaller* runs must be done. Instead of doing 100,000 dozen items in one run, as they do with independent classifications, with related separates they'll do, say, 2,000 dozen runs of one item, then 2,000 dozen of another, and so on. This means they have to stop their machines after each item's production, then start all over again on a new item. In the Orient, a manufacturer automatically pays a premium on smaller runs. That, too, gets figured into the final price.

Finally, a duty must be paid on any merchandise that is imported, and this too gets passed on to the consumer. There are two kinds of duty: low duty and high duty. A basic piece of wearing apparel, with no frills—just a simple garment, functionally equipped to make it work the way it should—is brought in at a low, or standard, duty. Anything that comes in with nonfunctional trim on it— fashion touches that are there for aesthetic purposes only—comes in at high duty. This is a significant part of what you'll be paying for.

Again, related separates are a concept, a convenience; but we want to reemphasize that what you are *not* paying for is just a shirt, a sweater, a jacket, or a pant. The per-unit cost will be higher on a related separates item than if you bought it in its parent department. Thus, the value is more perceived than actual—you see everything right in front of you, color-coordinated and fully related, and that aesthetic compatibility makes the package *look* good.

We still feel that you should look for all the quality features in related separates that you would look for in any individual item of apparel. Just be aware of what goes into the pricing of related separates and you will be able to make a sounder value judgment when you purchase them.

8. Apparel Accessories

UNDERWEAR, hosiery, belts, and shoes are obviously important items in most men's lives, yet there is perhaps no other area of menswear that receives as perfunctory and unimaginative attention as apparel accessories. This is particularly true of underwear and hosiery, because of their highly functional and largely hidden nature. We believe far too many men think of underwear and socks as dull but necessary items, best bought on sale.

Underwear and socks, by virtue of the role they play in our wardrobes, are too important to be relegated to the sales bins full-time. These are the items of apparel that touch your skin most directly, the foundation upon which everything else you wear rests.

Shoes are obviously important in your wardrobe, because they protect your feet from the elements as well as from the daily pressure and stress of having to transport the entire weight of your body. Thus, as with outerwear, fashion must take a back seat to proper construction for a shoe to represent true quality. If you purchase a sloppily made shirt, you'll mostly *look* bad—a poorly constructed pair of shoes can make you *hurt*.

Accessories, then, play much more than a merely ancillary role in your wardrobe: They protect you, as well as the other items in your wardrobe. Accessories can lend to, or detract from, your physical and mental well-being. Comfort and ultimate serviceability are probably more important to these items of apparel than they are to any other area of menswear. So let's take the classifications of men's apparel accessories individually and determine how to recognize the highest level of quality in each.

UNDERSHIRTS AND UNDERSHORTS

Don't think of your underwear as a hidden layer of apparel, but as the first layer upon which a quality wardrobe is built. The style—boxer or briefs—is purely a personal decision, but to buy quality in either, you should address fabric, construction, and fit.

Fabric

Fabric should be the foremost consideration when you shop for underwear, if only because your underwear is the first layer of clothing you put against your skin when you dress.

Nature's way of helping you maintain your body temperature and a proper balance of body fluid is perspiration. When you perspire, that moisture has to go *somewhere*, and unless you run around nude all the time, that somewhere is into your clothing. Specifically, it is absorbed by your underclothing. For this reason, a fabric's breathability becomes an important consideration. You want a fabric that will keep you both dry and cool.

Nothing serves this purpose better than cotton. Cotton's high porosity makes it an ideal fabric for underwear; in fact, for a great many years nothing but all-cotton was used for men's underclothing. Cotton is also the most comfortable underwear fabric to wear, but in pure-finish form it still presents the same problem it does in other items of apparel—it has poor shape-retention properties and wrinkles dreadfully. In order to really look good, all cotton garments should be ironed after each laundering. But, needless to say, few of us have either the time or the desire to iron our underwear before we wear it.

The introduction of polyester to underwear brought the same properties it did to other pure-finish garments: better shape retention and lower price. But poly/cotton underwear does not breathe as well as all-cotton underwear, nor does it absorb perspiration as readily. This means that some of the moisture is trapped between your skin and the garment. So, the tradeoff is obvious: better prices and easier maintenance, or greater comfort. Some men can sense virtually no difference between all-cotton and the poly/cotton blends; for others the difference is objectionably obvious. Only *you* will know whether you can comfortably wear poly/cotton underclothing. If you tend to perspire heavily, this, too, should be a consideration.

Nylon is a third fabric that has become quite popular for underwear. It began in Europe, a number of years ago, as bikini swimwear that doubled as underwear. The reasoning behind this idea was that nylon dries more quickly than cotton, and can be washed out easily. Another factor was nylon's heaviness. It is heavier than cotton, with better shape retention. Also, the fact that this nylon is woven, and not knitted, meant that it offered more support.

The fact that nylon was more colorfast than all-cotton, and can be printed in more colorful ways, also accounted for its popularity. With the dual purpose it served as both swimwear and underwear, along with the wider variety of patterns and colors it could be offered in, the idea was met with a great deal of enthusiasm in the United States. What really sold was the fashion angle—and from a historical perspective, underwear was the last major classification of menswear to respond to fashion innovation. Perhaps this was due to the fact that, as we've said, most men have always regarded undergarments as purely functional items. Nonetheless, it is nylon we have to thank, or blame, for fashionable underwear.

Nylon's quick-drying, shape-retention, and color-taking qualities must, however, be balanced against its drawback: It virtually does not breathe, which can lead to and even encourage a number of hygienic problems, since perspiration sticks to the fabric instead of being absorbed by it.

So, again, the trade-off here is one of fashion versus function. If fashion underwear is a major statement for you, then nylon can't be beaten. But keep in mind that much more fashion coloring is now being done in all-cotton briefs—though the pattern diversity can never come close to nylon.

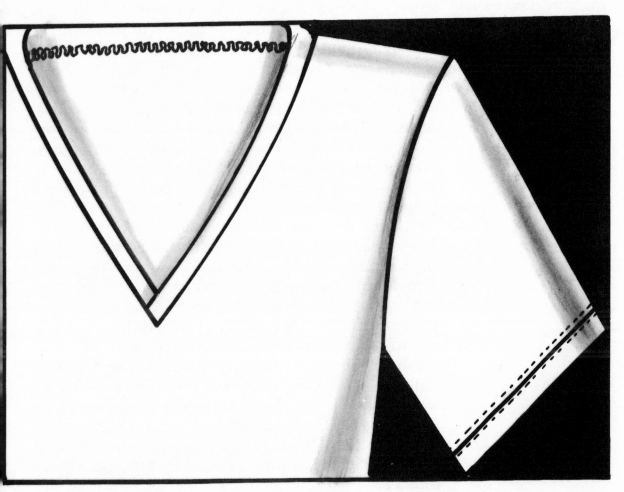

1. Smooth seams with no puckering.
2. Tight stitching.
3. Seams cleanly finished.

Construction Proper construction of underwear is crucial to quality, since construction contributes directly to proper fit, as well as to how the garments will hold up after being machine-washed and dried many, many times. Also, no other garment comes into closer contact with your body and its direct movement than underwear. The two key elements in underwear construction, therefore, are how the garments were sewn, and the quality of the elastic used in them. Generally speaking, the tighter both the elastic and the stitching are, the better constructed the garments are.

First, the stitching. Underwear undergoes a tremendous amount of stress, from wearing to washing to drying and wearing again. The chances of unraveling are greater in underclothing than in any other garment you own. For that reason, stitching must be tight and strong.

Tight elastic is also crucial in undershorts, whether you wear boxers or briefs. In briefs, the elastic has to be durable enough to fit snugly but comfortably around your waistline and the upper parts of your thighs. It must be durable enough to spring right back to its original shape after it has been washed and dried.

The elastic performs the same function at the waistline in boxer shorts, but there *is* a bit of difference. Boxer shorts are usually made from a woven broadcloth finished fabric, while briefs are made of knitted fabric. The shrinkage factor is greater in knits than it is in woven fabric, and so when you buy briefs (except those in nylon), the entire brief, elastic included, will shrink when washed.

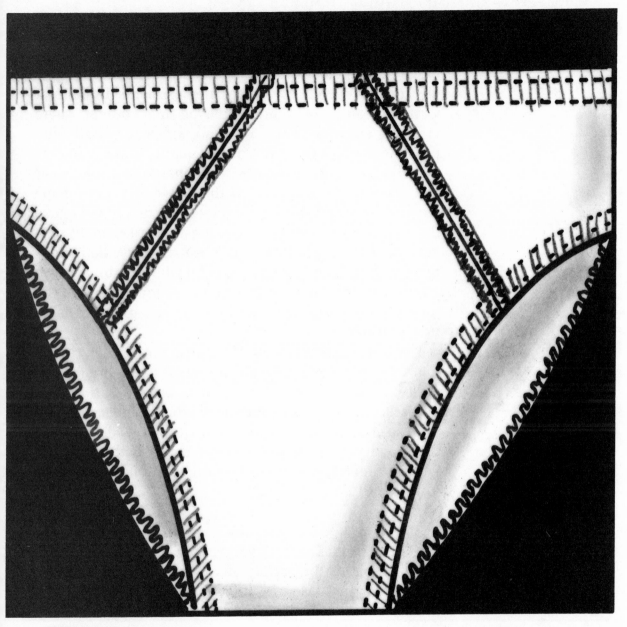

1. Pieced crotch.
2. Tight elastic for shape retention.

Since the vast majority of underwear sold is displayed in prepackaged cellophane, how can the consumer really judge these elements of quality? Many stores will probably have removed several of the garments from their wrappers, and have them displayed on a counter where you can examine them. Even so, since it is still only possible to judge the construction quality of the garments visually, you may just have to purchase them first, wear and wash them, and then, if they have lost their shape after one or two washes, or if they begin to unravel—take them back to the store and request a replacement or a refund. If the replacement is unsatisfactory, *demand* a refund. Returns may seem a great deal of trouble, but we assure you they will be less of an inconvenience in the long run than paying for and living with uncomfortable undergarments.

The last crucial element of construction, which relates to briefs, is the pouch area. All better-quality briefs have a set-in panel that forms the pouch, providing the room necessary for comfort. One-piece fabric panels, running from seam to seam with no pouch allowance, do not have this much-needed quality factor. Briefs with one-piece fabric panels only exist because they are less expensive to make.

Fit The fit of underwear is very much a personal matter, which explains the variety of styles in both undershorts and undershirts. Men have different feelings about how much fabric they want against their skin, and how tightly it should fit. Whatever your preference, make certain the garments fit exactly as you want them to. If you buy underwear—briefs in particular—that is too tight, you are doing yourself a disservice through discomfort, and you're doing the garment a disservice by forcing the elastic to stretch beyond its intended limits.

Similarly, undershirts that are too tight will have undue stress placed upon them in the shoulder area, which will encourage the stitching to come undone. Also, an undershirt that is too tight under the arm will restrict movement and create extreme discomfort in that area.

On the other hand, a garment that is overly full in fit is no bargain either. The fullness will add bulkiness beneath your clothing, disrupting the natural silhouette each garment was designed to have.

HOSIERY

For many years, there was only one story to tell in hosiery, and that was yarn content. Socks were always made from pure fibers, and different fibers were used for different purposes. Fine-quality wool was the standard for dress socks, and cotton worked well for casual wear. All-silk socks (which are still available) were the ultimate.

The reason pure-finish yarns were used in hosiery is obvious: the breathability of the fiber. This breathability factor is essential in hosiery. The drawback with pure-finish yarns in socks, however, as it was with underwear in general until the Sanforizing process reduced the problem, was shrinkage.

A revolution took place in the hosiery industry with the introduction of nylon and acrylic. Nowhere in menswear was the introduction of synthetics more successful than in hosiery. Nylon as a fiber has several distinct advantages. First, it is lightweight—much lighter than either wool or cotton. Second, nylon has better elasticity qualities than cotton or wool—an important factor to consider, especially with over-the-calf socks, which are meant to stay up. Nylon also washes and dries quite well, and shrinkage is practically nonexistent.

True, nylon does not possess the breathability of natural fibers, but this is not really an issue in hosiery, because only *featherweight* nylon is used. So, in dress socks, you can't really make a quality judgment on the basis of natural fiber versus synthetic fiber. Each has a validity of its own, and you must decide what each is worth based on your own needs.

Strictly from a fashion standpoint, nylon is rarely dyed in the variety of colors that cotton or wool are, and so the color range in nylon is very limited when compared to what you can get in cotton or wool. In terms of durable elasticity, a nylon sock is really the best for holding up wash after wash, drying after drying. And good elasticity is vital in a sock because of the daily stress it must contend with. A sock must necessarily be stretched totally out of shape, molding to the shape of your foot, and stay that way for as long as you have it on.

Today, many sock manufacturers have successfully blended natural fibers with synthetic fibers in order to produce both dress and sport socks. This marriage has resulted in the birth of a sock that offers the comfort of natural fiber and the durability of synthetic.

It is worth repeating that any sock, to represent quality, must have good elasticity, and this is especially true where dress socks are concerned. The best-quality socks have an extra-tight elastic around the top that pulls the fiber even closer together. Most dress socks have very tight ribbing, and the quality of the ribbing has a great

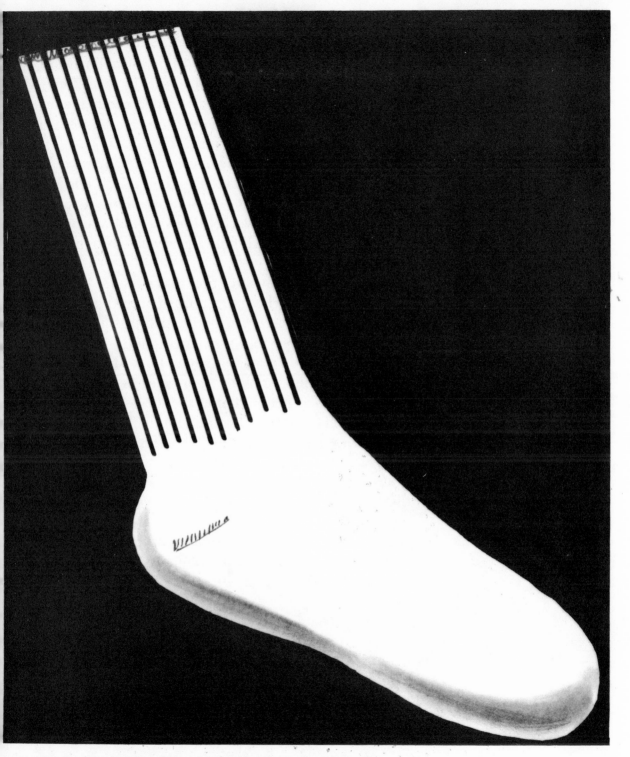

1. Sport socks—tight ribbing with tight elastic spring-back.
2. Elastic reinforcement at top of sock.

deal to do with the way the sock will perform. Be aware, however, that different types of socks have different types of ribbing. Sport socks that rest just above the ankles have little in common with over-the-calf dress socks when it comes to ribbing.

When you look at a sock, the elastic might appear to be tight—but take it in your hands, pull it apart, and see how quickly it springs back to its original shape. Remember that after you have worn the sock, and washed it several times, it should still hold up as well as on the first day you wore it.

Two other areas to pay attention to are the toe and the heel reinforcements. These are knitted into the sock itself, and most manufacturers distinguish this by using a different-color yarn so that you can actually see that it has been done. It's an excellent sign of quality, because, except for your thigh area, nowhere else is more stress placed on undergarments than at the toe and the heel.

Fitting a sock is actually quite simple. Socks are offered either in specific sizes or in the form of one-size-fits-all. Traditionally, before nylon, all hosiery was sized. All-cotton, all-wool, and all-silk socks are still sized. All synthetic socks, however, are one-size-fits-all.

To actually say that one is better than the other is difficult, because it is actually unnecessary to give nylon socks exact sizing. On the other hand, the proportionate sizing of cotton, wool, and silk socks does offer a better fit.

SHOES   As we noted earlier, shoes do a great deal more for you than merely dress up your feet or protect them from the elements. Shoe support your feet, and your feet support

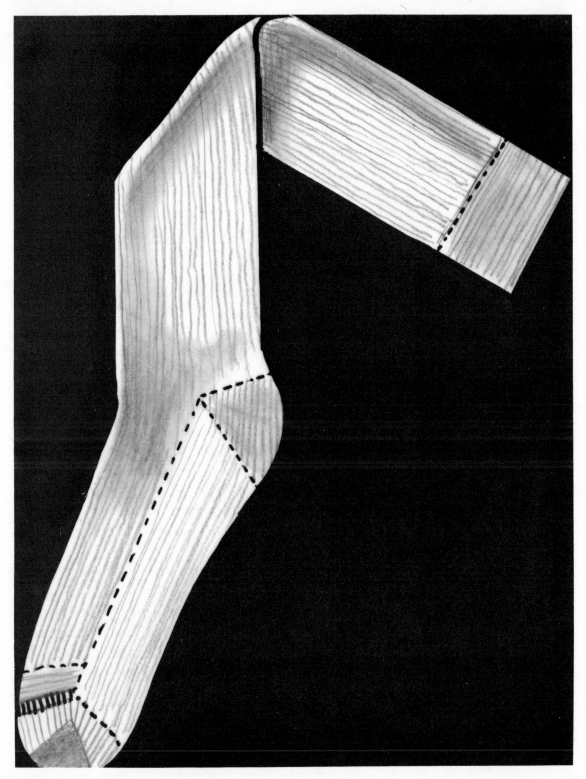

1. *Tight elastic ribbing—especially at top.*
2. *Reinforced heel and toe (major stress points).*

the weight of your entire body. Keep in mind that each time you take a step, your weight is slammed into your feet; when you are simply standing still your feet are still hard at work because they each continue to support half of your total weight.

Your feet are your body's shock absorbers. Poorly constructed shoes, or shoes that don't fit correctly, will not only hamper this service your feet render but also contribute to numerous and disparate health problems, from corns and calluses to lower-back pain. Shoddily constructed shoes will also cause pain in your pocket, because they will fall apart much sooner than they should, considering the rather significant sum of money charged for most shoes today.

When you shop for a quality shoe, the three key areas to concentrate on are construction, material, and fit. Don't let function take a back seat to fashion. Shop with the thought that your shoes must protect your feet first; then they may be trendy, interesting, or unusual in design and color. We feel strongly that designers who place visual interest over proper construction in their shoes, and the manufacturers who make them, should be forced to wear those shoes twenty-four hours a day. We doubt, however, that they wear them at all—and neither should you.

Construction　It would take an entire book to tell you all there is to know about quality shoe construction. Over two hundred steps go into bringing a shoe from its unformed state to its final shape. Though we can't spell them all out for you, we *can* arm you with the basics and let you take it from there.

1. Shape of shoe essential to proper fit.
2. Tight, even stitching throughout.

There are three basic shoe constructions to choose from: *cement* construction, *moccasin* construction, and *welt* construction.

In cement construction, a very thin outer sole is cemented directly to an "upper," along with an insole. There's very little between you and the ground, which means this type of shoe is not ideal for walking on pavement.

A moccasin also has only a thin leather outer sole, which is hand-sewn along the top of the shoe. Though moccasins are generally worn for sport, some men do choose them for dress wear. They really aren't best for walking, or for being on your feet a great deal.

Welt construction is the quality way to make a shoe, and also a very old way. In this method, a thick outsole is sewn onto an upper.

In terms of overall construction quality, a good shoe really begins with a well-thought-out design concept. Shoes are the only item of apparel that cannot be altered after they are made. Therefore, the first prerequisite for a quality shoe must be a well-thought-out last, the basic form around which a shoe is made. It is an unfortunate fact that a good number of lasts on the market today are not well thought out at all, but are designed for looks only. A shoe should obviously look good, but it is imperative that it fit well also. In terms of the shape of a shoe, there are several key areas to focus on to ascertain the quality of construction, and how the shoe will fit.

First, a telltale sign of a cheap shoe is a fat back. You want a narrow back in a shoe, and here's why. Take your shoe off and look at your bare foot. Specifically, note the way your instep area is made: There is no flesh in the instep or at the back of your heel. The reason a lot of shoe

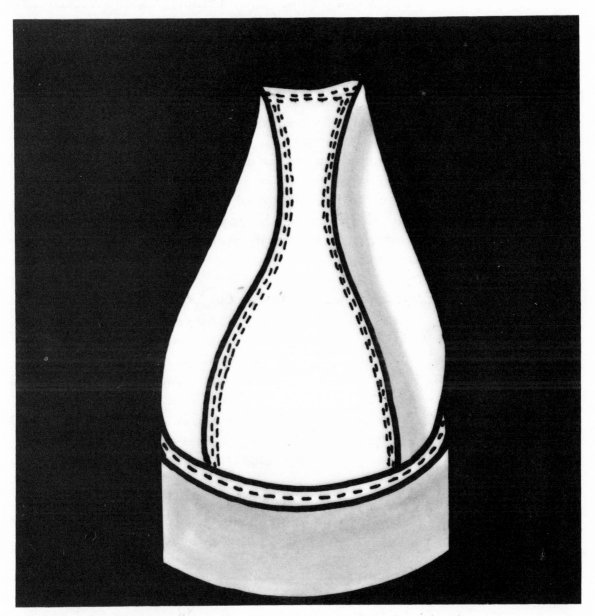

1. Heel construction narrower at top.
2. Heel panel inset—an extra quality touch.

manufacturers don't offer a properly narrow-backed shoe is that it takes time and effort; it is simply cheaper to make a fat-backed shoe. Also, few consumers are really aware of the need for a narrower back in a shoe, and so manufacturers simply don't bother offering it. Now you know, so look for it.

In a cheap shoe, because the back is too fat, your foot will slide forward. Then, if there isn't enough toe room up front, your big toe will hit the last, and you'll start to get a pressure point on that joint. Also, if the back part of the shoe is too high, it will dig into your foot and create a callus. This occurs because the manufacturer has over-constructed (it's simply easier), but there should never be extra material where you have so much bone and so little flesh.

You should also avoid shoes that are too oval in shape, because they will cause the toes and bones to be crushed inward. Too much of an oval shape will diminish the amount of room you need across the toe and the ball. It is a fact that if you measure your bare foot without standing on it and then measure it while standing, you'll pick up an extra half to three-fourths of an inch. When you stand on your foot it flattens out, so a quality shoe is usually quite a bit broader across the ball area, and generally not so high.

The quality of material is as important as construction. One of the first prerequisites is a leather insole. The synthetics used for this purpose today burn the feet, partly because of their diminished absorption and breathability properties. Leather is also best because it conforms better to the shape of your foot. Turn the shoe over and look at the bottom. It will usually tell you if the insole is of leather or synthetic.

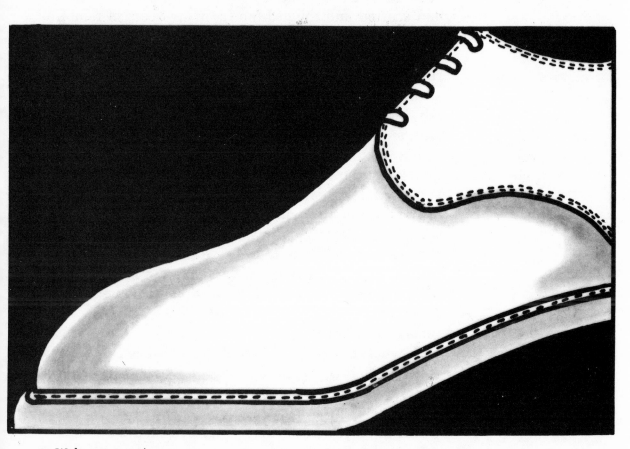

1. Welt construction.
2. *Make sure top of shoe comfortably accommodates foot.*

The weight of a shoe, in many cases, will indicate the degree of quality. A leather process commonly used in men's shoes is "corrected grain," the result of which is a very heavy leather. In this process, the manufacturer takes the hide of a big old cow or bull, naturally marred and scarred and tough from its many years of rambling through brambles and into barbed-wire fences, and tries to turn it into the proverbial silk purse. First a buffer is run across the surface of the leather in order to get rid of all the imperfections. When all the grain has been literally buffed off, it is painted, then plated, or stamped, with a new grain. It's a lifeless kind of leather, with the feel of oilcloth, and if you scrape or scuff it you'll immediately hit the white stuff—the underlayer—since there is really no epidermis there.

The best-quality material is called aniline leather, which is subjected to none of the above-mentioned "correcting" steps. A penetrating stain is simply put on the natural hide, and all of the original grain is left intact.

Finally, there is the matter of how a shoe should be sized. Since few of us can afford to have our shoes made precisely to the shape of our feet, we have to make do with what the shoe stores offer. Shoes come in sizes that are indicated by length and width. The length is designated by number (such as 9 or 9½), width by a letter or group of letters. Most shoe widths run A to E. The A width is narrow, but there is an even narrower width, AA. Double Es and triple Es are the widest widths available in men's shoes.

Regardless of what you *think* your shoe size is, to get the best fit you must have the salesperson measure your foot. This, of course, is a matter of routine in reputable shoe stores. If they don't measure your foot, and you don't particularly feel like walking out and finding another, more reputable shop, simply demand that your foot be measured. Actually, you should have *both* feet measured. Sometimes, indeed often, one foot is slightly larger than the other. If the size difference is considerable, you will have to try shoes on with special care to achieve the best compromise between too tight on one foot and too loose on the other.

Don't stop at having your feet measured. Put the shoes on and walk around in them. Check for all of the construction elements we told you about that relate to fit. Varying styles and shapes of shoes will fit differently, so take this into account. Is there room to move your toes around comfortably in those shoes? Are they wide enough so that your feet aren't crushed inward?

Do not be intimidated by the salesperson, or timid about sending the shoes back and asking for another size, shape, or even color in that same size and style, if you aren't happy with them once you see them on your feet.

Lastly, two facts about shopping for shoes—one a myth, the other a hint. First, forget anything you ever heard about having to "break in" a shoe to make it fit the way it should. When a salesperson tells you that you have to break a shoe in, what he's really telling you is that, with time, you have to wait for your *foot* to conform to the *shoe*. Rubbish. A shoe should fit when you first put it on the way it should when you've worn it for years. A good shoe, properly fitted, will.

Second, a valuable tip we've discovered over a period of time: Try not to shop for shoes on a day when you have already "walked your feet off." Feet *swell* when they've been overused, and you will not get the most accurate fit.

BELTS A belt is one of the few items in a man's wardrobe that is adjustable. Even so, it must contend with a great deal of stress; while you're wearing it, it is essentially pulling in. But don't think of a belt as something intentionally designed to pull in more than it has to, or to contend with more stress than it should. A belt shouldn't cinch. Its functional purpose is to give the fit of your pant additional support. The ordinary amount of stress it must contend with is compounded by the fact that you are wearing it in the center of your body.

The two basic materials used in making belts are leather and fabric. Leather is generally used for dress belts, fabric for sportier models. (Suede is also used, but it tends to be highly perishable.)

Leather Usually, the leather that goes into a belt must be strong enough to withstand constant yanking through the buckle. For a long time, only a few types of leather were used in making belts: what the industry called belting leather. They are durable and stiff, and lend themselves well to the purpose.

We feel, though, that the best leather for a belt is one that is soft and pliable. We don't mean glove leather, but something in between. If you crush it slightly in your hand and let go, it should spring back to its original shape. Avoid overly stiff leather in a belt—usually an indication that the manufacturer used very cheap steerhide and glazed it. It will have an attractive, highly polished appearance, but eventually this boardlike leather will crack.

We suggest a belt of calfskin or top-grain cowhide, both of which offer pliability and suppleness, which means a belt that will hold up and wear longer.

One of the crucial construction elements in a quality belt is tight, uniform *machine* stitching. The tighter the stitches, the better. Some sportier belts have more widely spaced stitching. It's a fashion touch that may *look* better, but in terms of construction it's a poorer value.

Another key to a quality belt is how it was lined. The underside will have been lined in leather—a separate piece, cut in the shape of the belt, and sewn onto the inside. A cheaper belt will not have this element of lining. What the manufacturer will often do is simply finish the suede side of the leather, but not put *another* piece of leather on the belt's underside.

Now examine the loop on the belt, beside the buckle. How is the loop attached? Is it anchored, or simply loose? Is it stitched on, or stapled? On a quality belt, on which the buckle is attached to the belt, there should be a small piece of leather on the underside, extending from where the buckle is attached, from an inch to an inch and a half, and then attached to the loop.

The buckle itself must be attached to the belt very, very firmly, because that is where the greatest amount of stress occurs. A fine-quality belt will have an additional piece of leather extending anywhere from half to three quarters of an inch that has been sewn onto the buckle to reinforce its anchoring. A piece of leather that has simply been turned through the buckle and stitched is less expensive.

Buckle holes are of paramount importance, because

there is no margin for error when they are put in. On a leather belt, the holes are punched through and must be perfect, because they can't be redone. There should be no scraggly strands of leather hanging down, or the point of the buckle will pull and wear down the hole. The hole should be neither too small nor too large, so that the point fits into and out of it easily. Test the holes in the store to make certain they were punched in cleanly.

We're believers in solid belt buckles. Whatever the metal is, it should be solid, and not hollow inside. A lot of "fashion" belt buckles are hollow, but they tend to break easily. Another buckle problem you might encounter is an anchor pin (the point) that has not been attached properly. This is particularly a problem with belts that have only an anchor hook. If this hook breaks off the buckle, that buckle is finished. You can't really test a belt buckle for weakness in this area, but if it breaks shortly after you have purchased the belt, return it.

Fabric Fabric belts have become quite popular for sportswear. Just keep in mind that you needn't expect the same level of construction in a fabric belt that you would in a leather or dress belt. You simply don't need it. Nor should you be paying the same price for a piece of fabric that you would for a piece of leather. Overconstruction in a fabric belt simply adds up to dollars unnecessarily spent.

Look for the same quality elements in the buckle; make sure the buckle holes are cleanly finished, and that any stitching on the belt has been done neatly and firmly.

In terms of fit, a belt is one piece of apparel that you

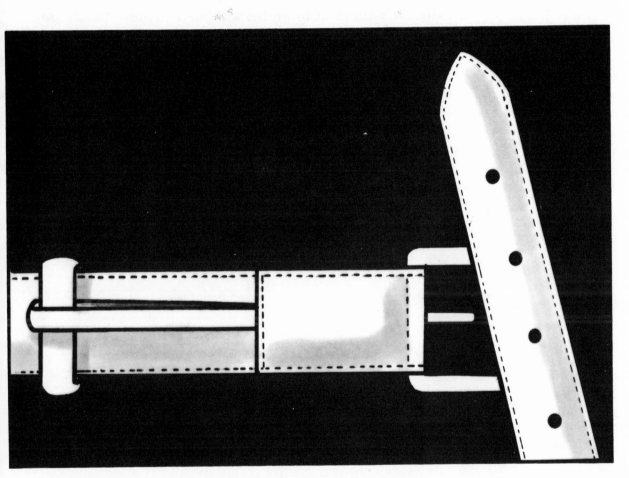

1. Added piece of leather behind buckle base to secure buckle
   more firmly and provide anchor for floating loop.

can try on in the store with no problem. In our opinion, the best place to close a belt is on the middle hole. If there are five holes on the belt, it should close, comfortably, on the third. Finally, when you close the belt, there should not be overlap of more than about 4 inches. Otherwise, the belt is too big.

9. How to Shop for Menswear

Now that we've talked about each component of menswear, we'd like to take some of the mystery out of shopping in general and the options on where to buy apparel. There are three types of retailers of menswear—specialty stores, department stores, and discount outlets—and we'd like to make you aware of the advantages and the disadvantages associated with shopping in each of them.

SPECIALTY STORES

For many years, when all men's clothing was tailor-made, the haberdasher was an institution in a man's life. With the advent of ready-made suits, shirts, and coats, the haberdasher evolved into the specialty store. Some specialty stores still maintain a custom-order or special-order department, but most today simply have merchandise ready to sell "off the rack."

Specialty stores offer several advantages to men—and a few disadvantages, but we definitely feel that the former far outweigh the latter.

The suit and sportcoat department of any specialty store usually has a much broader inventory of merchandise than a conventional department store, so you're offered a much wider selection.

A second advantage of specialty stores is that their sales personnel are better trained, which means they usually have much more information at hand about the merchandise they are selling. Thus the consumer is better served.

A salesperson in a specialty store can, in fact, outfit you totally, taking you from the suit department to the shirt department to the tie department, and so on. This permits the salesperson to assist you in creating a totally coordinated look. By contrast, the salespeople in most department stores rarely leave their own department, so you're basically on your own when it comes to putting a total wardrobe package together.

If you shop regularly in one particular specialty store, and establish a close relationship with one specific salesperson, that person will serve you better by keeping a customer card file on you. That file will list what you have purchased in the past, colors, sizes, patterns, and what your preferences are. Thus when you go into the store, you are not walking in as a stranger, but as someone with whom that store representative has an ongoing relationship. The salesperson can then serve you better, more efficiently, and more quickly.

Another word about specialty-store salespeople. Most are paid on the basis of some form of commission; they earn according to what they sell. Thus, because the more they sell the more they earn, they tend to have a considerably different attitude than sales "clerks," who are paid the same amount whether they produce or not.

However, any professional salesperson also knows that if he is to build a client relationship with you, you must be happy with what you have purchased, which of course will bring you back for more. If that salesperson "sells" you an item of questionable value, or fit, you will remember it, and not return. Good salespeople are worth their weight in gold, because of their ability to save you time and understand your taste level. The salesperson acts as your own private counselor and fashion coordinator. Find one you like, and your life will be made much, much easier when you shop.

A third important advantage to shopping in specialty stores is the quality they offer in alteration. In tailored clothing, appearance is crucial. As we've said, a suit must fit you well or it is a waste of money. Generally, alterations in a specialty store are better because the only alterations they do are on menswear—the tailors, pressers, and seamstresses work on menswear and nothing else. The construction of menswear, particularly in tailored apparel, is considerably different from that of women's and children's apparel. All things considered, we believe that you'll get a better-fitting suit from the tailoring shop in a specialty store than you will in a department store.

The disadvantages of specialty stores vary from store to store, of course, but some generalizations can be made.

To begin with, the credit, return, and refund policies may not be as lenient as they will be in department stores. Department stores will refund virtually any purchase.

The cost of running an in-house credit department has forced many specialty stores to abandon in-house credit policies and use bank credit or other credit cards only. Further, many specialty stores have stricter policies on returns—while, again, department stores tend to be more liberal in this case.

One other potential disadvantage of shopping in a specialty store can stem from one of the advantages we mentioned earlier: involved salespeople. Your ability to amble and browse about freely might be hampered. Some customers just want to walk around and browse without being encumbered by salespeople; they just want to *shop*. There are some specialty stores where, because of store layout and the number of salespeople, casual browsing is difficult and sometimes impossible.

One last area of comparison between specialty stores and other types of retailers is that of price. Specialty stores with beautiful wood paneling and luxurious carpeting— some even serve their customers drinks and otherwise pamper them—are more expensive. Having a battalion of salespeople costs money, as do the other amenities specialty stores offer to make shopping a pleasure. These costs are reflected in the overall markup on the merchandise. All those things are nice if you don't mind paying for them; just make sure you're getting them!

DEPARTMENT STORES

Department stores are far more than just carriers of merchandise. In many cities they are institutions, much like a museum, a symphony orchestra, or the Fourth of July parade. Indeed, many department stores throughout the country take great pride in their community achievements and in the civic responsibilities they meet. For many years department stores were known for carrying a wide range of merchandise that appealed to many taste levels, and they gave the customer a great deal of service.

Today, very few department stores are owned by the original founding families. Indeed, most are owned by large groups like Federated Department Stores, May Department Stores Company, Associated Dry Goods Company, Allied Stores, and Carter, Hawley Hale, to name but a few. The board of directors of each of these companies has to report to stockholders, who expect a profit at the end of the fiscal year—and let there be no mistake about it, profit is the name of the game.

Let's look at the plus side of department-store shopping first. From the start, department stores serve the entire community, and therefore have a much broader range of customers than specialty stores do. By the nature of today's lifestyles, sportswear has become a major component in every man's wardrobe—and department stores have increasingly made sportswear their forte. Not because they like sportswear, but because the inventory turn (the rate at which a store's invested dollars in inventory is rolled over) is much greater in this area than it is in tailored apparel. Sportswear also requires less sales help to move it, because less fitting is involved.

Another excellent reason for shopping in department stores is the value you get on specific items. Most department stores belong to very organized buying offices, and buying offices are able to purchase specific items in bulk, at a much lower price than if the individual store tried to purchase it. It stands to reason that the price of item X is going to be less when 10,000 dozen are being ordered than when only 1,000 dozen are ordered.

Many department-store buying offices are spread throughout the world, and their staff go immediately to the best places for the best values. In fact, many buying offices put together their own programs, through color, pattern, and fabric, with manufacturers in order to create items that are exclusively theirs. The merchandise, then, becomes a much better value, and the savings are usually passed on to the consumer at the store level.

Yet another good reason to shop in department stores is, as we mentioned earlier, their liberal credit and return policies. All stores want satisfied customers, and one way of ensuring that is to let you know that if you don't like the item you bought, you can get a refund on it. Liberal credit policies also make it easy to open store charge accounts, and buying now and paying later is an appealing prospect these days.

One final reason for shopping in department stores is that they're *fun*. Stanley Goodman, former chairman of the board of the May Department Stores Company, once said that department stores should be "living theaters." Many department stores make themselves just that, creating an aura of excitement about themselves that makes them a focal point of activity. Department stores can have the most exciting special events, they can sponsor community activities—in short, they lure you in in much the same way that street bazaars have lured in shoppers for centuries. There's just a hell of a lot going on.

Perhaps no area of American retailing has undergone **DISCOUNT** such a dramatic change in the past ten years as the dis- **STORES** count-store concept. From their humble origins, offering odd lots, irregulars, and old or distressed merchandise, discount stores have attained a level of considerable status through the quality of their merchandise. Many discount stores today proudly advertise the "latest" in designer names, brands, and current merchandise that is selling at much higher prices in the "uptown" stores.

To get real values from a discount store, however, it is best to have a clear idea of what you're after, and to be able to recognize the elements of quality that go into any garment (a skill we hope you have by now).

First, how do they do it? How can many discount stores buy current merchandise, in season, and sell it at discount? Here's how. If a manufacturer can be guaranteed a large cutting of piecegoods, for any piece of merchandise, that manufacturer will take the order. Even if the profit is lower per garment, it is still worthwhile for the manufacturer to fill an order from a discount store for, say, 1,000 units than to expend the time and effort trying to sell 200 units each to five different retailers. Additionally, if a conventional specialty store or department store cancels an order because it is a week late, many discount stores will take it—at a considerable reduction in wholesale cost; the manufacturer is simply happy to get rid of it.

There are even times when a discount store can go to a manufacturer and pay the *same* price as any other store—

but since the discount store's overhead is so much lower than that of conventional stores, it can still offer the merchandise at considerably lower prices. This is, in fact, the "no frills" policy that allowed many discounters to go into business in the first place.

Generally, discount stores offer very little in terms of amenities and services. There is virtually no sales help around, and no atmosphere to speak of; the store is usually just a cavernlike structure with lots of pipe racks. Advertising is also kept to a minimum, and is only price-oriented in nature. Discounters claim, and rightly, that you aren't going to *wear* the "frills," so why should you pay for them? That, of course, is a question of personal preference. You don't eat the flowers on the table at a restaurant, but most people would agree that their presence does make the dinner more enjoyable.

Since there is little sales help available to you in a discount store, you'll be totally on your own when you shop there. You'll be alone in finding the garment, alone in trying it on, and for the most part alone in answering any questions you may have about it. Because of the very nature of these stores, it is difficult to put a total outfit together with the ease you'd have in a conventional store. Specialty stores have the service; department stores have the fixtures and easy-flow floor plans from one department to another. Discount stores have none of these. So, if you have the time, the interest, and the basic ability to put an outfit together on your own, go for it.

One other tip we'd like to give you about discount-store shopping has to do with price comparisons. We advise you to scrutinize any store's price comparisons carefully. Be wary of claims that a suit at, say, $150 is comparable to suits selling "uptown" for $300. Ask yourself: Is it really the same garment, or is it just similar? If it is similar, *how* is it similar—in pattern? fabric? color? construction? When you discount-shop, make doubly certain the ads keep their promises. All too often, that $150 suit is worth only $150!

Department and specialty stores traditionally held their major sales at the end of the selling season, in order to clean out merchandise and make room for newly arriving items for the forthcoming season. During the normal selling season there may have been an occasional special event, but the major selling of marked-down merchandise was definitely at the *end* of that season. This merchandise was from the store's regular stock, sold all season long at regular price, and now offered at reductions. It was a legitimate value, and customers flocked to these events. **SALES AND STORE PROMOTIONS**

Today the end-of-season clearance as the *main* sale period is a thing of the past. It seems that stores are having sales and promotions almost every week, to the point that consumers have legitimately begun to wonder what is *really* on sale.

In some stores it is almost impossible to buy anything at *regular* price. Sales today are strategically planned events, and the merchandise offered at these events is planned as well. Lest the reader assume a conspiracy is afoot, we hasten to add that these planned events may well offer values on merchandise worth buying. But you should always look carefully into any sales event before you dive into one.

Look at the event itself; see what the ad copy announcing it has to say. Find out whether the merchandise being offered is from regular stock, is a special purchase, or is part of a storewide sales event.

We feel that the most legitimate sale is one in which merchandise from the regular stock has been reduced. But even here caution is advised. Many stores bring in stock—especially in import programs—at a low price, and mark it intentionally high with the specific intention of marking it down later. These stores know that even with this markdown, such stock will still be making a significant profit—so that whatever is sold at the higher markup simply adds to their gross margin.

A standard vehicle for this high markup and later reduction is the store label, or a special label the store uses as a promotional vehicle. This private-label program separates the merchandise from anything similar that a competitor may be carrying. Any consumer knows that if a garment has a brand label or designer label in it, a store must keep the price on that garment as close as possible to what the competitor down the street is charging. Private-label merchandise is a different story.

Stores today have become very sophisticated in their development of several house labels. One may be a vehicle for merchandise that is bought for the express purpose of "sale." Another may be merchandise that will be sold at regular price throughout the season, to be marked down only at the season's end. The labels may or may not have the store name on them.

We urge you to become acquainted with store labels, particularly if you shop at one store regularly, so that you understand what the purpose of that label is. If the label is unfamiliar to you, do not hesitate to ask the salesperson what it means. Is it a new brand? A new designer? Is it a store label? Ask questions; you have a right to know.

In short, approach all sales with your eyes open. Do not assume a value is there simply because price comparisons are made. Indeed, be wary of stores that are constantly on "sale." If they are constantly on sale, then their *sale* price becomes their *regular* price—and then the value of the merchandise itself is questionable. If you follow our guidelines to quality in any garment, you should be able to know the value of any item regardless of what its price tag says about it.

HOW TO TALK TO STORE EMPLOYEES

Nothing is more frustrating than trying to get information out of a salesperson who is either surly, uninterested, uninformed, or a combination of all three. Salespeople are there to assist you—you, the person spending the money.

The proficiency levels of salespeople do, of course, vary, depending upon the store in which they work. We feel that, generally, the best salespeople are found in specialty stores. As we said earlier, they are usually the best informed and most knowledgeable. They know the products they sell and how to sell them with superior service; they work on commission.

One thing to remember when speaking with salespeople is not to be intimidated. They are there to look after your needs, not vice versa. If you've read the preceding chapters in this book, you know much more about quality than most of the salespeople in either department or specialty stores. However, if there's something you don't know, ask; you have a right to an answer. And if a salesperson doesn't have the answer, suggest, politely, that he or she go and find out.

Ask pertinent, direct questions about the product; avoid playing "games" with the salesperson. Always be as specific as possible. Remember that when you ask a qualitative or value-judgment question, you are asking for an opinion, and not a specific answer to a specific question (i.e., "How much will it shrink?").

WORKING WITH A TAILOR

The key store employee who will make a garment look good on you is the tailor. The tailor is the equivalent of a surgeon for apparel. His success in making the garment fit you as well as possible will determine how good you look in it.

A good tailor knows more about the garment he is working with than you will ever know. He or she has been trained for years to know how to alter a garment, how certain fabrics respond to pressing, and, of course, how a garment was made. Even though you are in his hands, you needn't be at a loss. At this point you should be armed with enough information about apparel construction to make intelligent comments and ask pertinent questions about the alterations being made on the suit or sportcoat or slacks you've just purchased.

Keep several things in mind, however. The tailor knows how much the cost to the store will be for tailoring the garment. He also probably has an excellent idea of how a specific alteration will come out; for example, lowering the back of a garment is much more complicated than, say, shortening sleeves. Don't let the tailor talk you out of an alteration if a suit is going to look unsatisfactory on you. On the other hand, if the tailor is suggesting *too many* extensive alterations, don't buy the suit. Ready-made clothing should fit as close to perfect as possible, with the fewest possible alterations.

While the tailor marks the suit, make sure to watch, in a three-way mirror—and by all means stand as you normally would. Don't, on the other hand, stand at attention.

Don't be in a hurry. Let the tailor take the time he needs to make the garment work right for you. You've just paid dearly for that garment—make sure it will serve you well. Take your time, and make sure the tailor takes his.

An important thing to remember about alterations is that any good store will allow you a "basted try-on." That is, once the alteration is made, the seams are basted, not sewn, so that you can try the suit on and see how it will look—*before* the final sewing is done. This is important, because if other alterations are necessary, the suit can be adjusted right then and there, rather than having the store finish the sewing and then have to rip out the seams again if the work is unsatisfactory.

Regardless of the nature of the alterations, remember that *you* know how you want the suit to fit. The tailor can't read your mind, so be direct and to the point in telling him.

Keep in mind, also, that cloth is not steel. The tailor is not adjusting a computer, a copy machine, or a typewriter. He is adjusting a piece of cloth that will undergo a considerable amount of stress when you wear it. So, after you have worn the suit several times, it may well need a small adjustment in fit. If so, take it back and have it done.

Index